TAKING OFF THE MASK

of related interest

Autism and Masking
How and Why People Do It, and the Impact It Can Have
Dr Felicity Sedgewick, Dr Laura Hull & Helen Ellis
ISBN 978 1 78775 579 6
eISBN 978 1 78775 580 2

Camouflage
The Hidden Lives of Autistic Women
Dr Sarah Bargiela
Illustrated by Sophie Standing
ISBN 978 1 78592 566 5
eISBN 978 1 78592 667 9

Pretending to be Normal
Living with Asperger's Syndrome (Autism Spectrum Disorder) Expanded Edition
Liane Holliday Willey
ISBN 978 1 84905 755 4
eISBN 978 0 85700 987 6

TAKING OFF THE MASK

Practical Exercises to Help Understand and Minimise the Effects of Autistic Camouflaging

Dr Hannah Louise Belcher

Foreword by Will Mandy, PhD, DClinPsy

Jessica Kingsley Publishers
London and Philadelphia

First published in Great Britain in 2022 by Jessica Kingsley Publishers
An imprint of Hodder & Stoughton Ltd
An Hachette Company

1

A CIP catalogue record for this title is available from the
British Library and the Library of Congress

ISBN 978 1 78775 589 5
eISBN 978 1 78775 590 1

Printed and bound in Great Britain by TJ Books Limited

Jessica Kingsley Publishers' policy is to use papers that are natural,
renewable and recyclable products and made from wood grown in
sustainable forests. The logging and manufacturing processes are expected
to conform to the environmental regulations of the country of origin.

Jessica Kingsley Publishers
Carmelite House
50 Victoria Embankment
London EC4Y 0DZ

www.jkp.com

This book is dedicated to all the autistic people I have met who taught me who I was and accepted me for who I am.

Contents

Foreword by Will Mandy, PhD, DClinPsy 9

Acknowledgements 11

Disclaimer 13

Introduction 15

1. Learning to Imitate 23

2. The Drive to Camouflage 35

3. Do You Camouflage? 61

4. How to Be Self-Compassionate 79

5. Taking Off the Mask 109

6. Final Thoughts 139

References 143

Further Reading 149

Subject Index 151

Author Index 153

Foreword

Autistic people generally find themselves living in situations that were designed by and for non-autistic people and, as such, they are commonly expected to live in ways that just do not fit with their needs and natural inclinations. Furthermore, people are often very unforgiving of those who do not conform to their social norms, and autistic people suffer from this all the time, as shown by the high rates of bullying that they continue to face. As Dr Hannah Louise Belcher explains, many autistic people seek to deal with this predicament using a collection of strategies that have come to be known as 'camouflaging', 'masking' and 'adaptive morphing', among other terms. This means they seek to hide their autistic traits in order to fit in, sometimes developing elaborate, energy-consuming repertoires of behaviour so they can 'pass' in their interactions with non-autistic people. As Dr Belcher explains, this autistic masking is a natural human response to the challenges of being autistic in a majority-non-autistic world, and can be useful in some situations, for example, during a job interview. But she also makes it very clear, both through relating her own experiences and by drawing on the latest scientific research, that masking is commonly harmful to autistic people, leaving many feeling exhausted, anxious, and unsure of their true wants and needs, let alone how to get these met.

One of the things I find so valuable about this book is that (almost uniquely among autism researchers) Dr Belcher actually has some practical, valid advice about how to address the situation. She acknowledges that masking is best understood as something that is imposed on autistic people by unaccommodating environments – we must not make the mistake of placing all responsibility for reducing masking on autistic individuals. Instead, we should ask how environments, such as schools and workplaces, can be made more inclusive so that they no longer impose the obligation to mask. Nevertheless, Dr Belcher is able to offer practical advice to autistic people on how they can reflect on their masking, and then use this as a starting point for gradually reducing it. In this process, there is potential for self-discovery and the prospect of a life that feels more authentic and satisfying.

Is there anyone better qualified to write this book on 'taking off the mask'? I don't think so. Dr Belcher is an academic psychologist who brilliantly articulates her own experiences of masking as an autistic girl and then woman, and of the subsequent journey she has been on creating a different way to be in the world. In this engaging and practical book, she draws upon her own life, her conversations with other autistic people, and disciplines including cognitive behavioural therapy, evolutionary psychology, cognitive neuroscience, and mindfulness. Her tone is compassionate, and she communicates clearly. The book is full of concrete advice and clear steps that can be taken and provides a range of worksheets to help people along.

This is an invaluable resource, providing authentic and wise advice on a topic for which, up to now, there has been little guidance. It is aimed at autistic readers but will be an essential resource for any professional working with autistic people. It tells the story of how Dr Belcher's determination, compassion and creativity have enabled her to discover her true self again, and will surely help guide many others on their own journeys in this direction.

Will Mandy, PhD, DClinPsy; Professor of
Neurodevelopmental Conditions, UCL, 2022

Acknowledgements

This book was inspired by conversations with Professor Will Mandy at University College London, who had recently written a paper entitled 'Social camouflaging in autism: is it time to lose the mask?' (Mandy 2019). I was also heavily influenced by other researchers who had found a link between camouflaging and poorer mental health in autistic people, such as Dr Sarah Cassidy and Dr Laura Hull. They helped me to better understand the need to provide mental health support for autistic people and informed my own research and PhD on the topic.

The ideas I had were shaped too by the other autistic people I spoke to or read about: those who had written and published their own experiences, those who contributed their valuable lived experiences to the pages of this book, and those who provided a listening ear while I was writing.

None of the practical and therapeutic ideas I have shared in this book would have been possible without some of the brilliant psychotherapists I have worked with over the years, especially my former art therapist, Diana Watts, who first recognised that I was autistic and opened up this world to me. I was also helped by the Adult Autism Psychological Therapies Service at the Maudsley Hospital, where I first learned techniques to reduce my camouflaging. I had the privilege of consulting with several psychotherapists while writing this book whom I wish to thank too, in particular clinical psychologist Dr Katherina Hamm.

Finally, I thank both my Mum, Linda Belcher, my wife, Megan Bennett, and my mother-in-law, Nicky Bennett, who spent time helping me to edit this book.

Disclaimer

Autism spectrum condition (formally known as autism spectrum disorder), is a neurodevelopmental condition with a wide array of traits and co-occurring conditions associated with it. As such, the autistic spectrum includes a diverse population of people who are all very different. What I have written in this book is my own understanding and perspective of being autistic, and therefore some may disagree with the ideas I present and the terminology I have used. This book uses the lived experience of other autistic people too, however, it's important to note that these views are coming from autistic people who do not have intellectual impairments. Many of us do, however, have co-occurring physical and mental health difficulties, but would be described, using old diagnostic terminology, as 'high-functioning' or having 'Asperger syndrome' at the time of our diagnoses. This book may therefore not be applicable to all autistic people.

This book should not be used in place of therapy but alongside mental health support from a trained professional. If you find reading any of the topics or attempting to complete any of the exercises too overwhelming, then please seek support. If you require urgent mental health support you can contact one of the crisis lines listed:

UK
Samaritans
Email: jo@samaritans.org
Phone: 116 123

USA
The National Suicide Prevention Lifeline
Phone: 1-800-273-8255
Online Chat: https://suicidepreventionlifeline.org

Australia
Lifeline
Text: 0477 13 11 14
Phone: 13 11 14

Introduction

To be a chameleon means being a person who changes their behaviours according to the situation they are in; it is a person who 'fits in' wherever they go – taken from the name of the chameleon lizard, a creature that can perform incredible changes to the colour of its skin in order to camouflage. However, it is a myth that chameleons camouflage to perturb their prey; rather their nervous system sends signals to the skin pigment mostly for social purposes (Stuart-Fox & Moussalli 2008). This spectacular array of colour change communicates its intentions to other chameleons; a bright colour can signal aggression while a darker colour can signal submission. These are automatic reactions, evolved over time to help chameleons operate their social landscape. Humans as a species may be socially more complex, but, as you will see over the next few chapters, we too have evolved a strategy that helps us to 'fit in' with those around us.

I have spent over a decade unravelling myself, carefully turning over each piece shattered on the floor since my first breakdown, desperate to find one that I could recognise. I realised I had been camouflaging my whole life, that is, I'd been trying to mask my autistic traits and fit in with all the non-autistic people around me, desperate to always be liked and to never draw attention to myself. Underneath was an abyss of emptiness, a stream of tainted thoughts that didn't belong to me. I was utterly lost, but little did I know that such a painful journey would lead to such an extraordinary rediscovery of myself and others.

My first day of school was full of tears and utter terror as I desperately tried to cry out for my mum to return and take me home. But I had no words. While the teachers would say I refused to talk, even at the age of four I knew this wasn't true. My words were stuck and I *couldn't* talk. Even when they waved a metaphorical carrot in front of my face, enticing me to give them a single word, I would shut down and nothing would come. A therapist attending the school also tried to prise the words out, explaining that I clearly could talk but was wilfully choosing not to. She was almost right, but what she was doing was so wrong. I didn't not talk because I was stubborn and wanted attention, quite the opposite. I didn't talk because of the all-consuming fear I had of exposing myself and creating *more* attention. Each word felt like I was revealing a new layer of my bare flesh. It became a vicious circle; not speaking shone a bigger and bigger spotlight over me, making me stand out from my peers and generating attention I did not want. So eventually I gave in. After my teacher had asked what picture I had drawn, with the accompanying prompt of "guinea...?" for what felt like the one-hundredth time, I squealed "pig" and sprinted off to the girls' toilets, thus beginning my lifelong goal of becoming a people pleaser.

I did such a good job at accomplishing this goal that I made it through school, college, and university before someone even contemplated that I might be autistic, myself included. I had written my entire undergraduate dissertation on why males are more likely to be autistic, and at no point had I reflected that I too had many of those traits and was struggling a great deal to conceal them. I knew something was throwing me off balance. I'd studied psychology at university, diagnosed myself with every possible psychiatric problem on the planet trying to figure out what was wrong with me, and autism had completely bypassed my radar. It wasn't until I started seeing an art therapist, who spotted my traits and explained how my anxiety was too consistently high and my difficulties too complex and longstanding to just be an anxiety disorder, that I realised. She had worked with me for over a year, and she understood me better than I had ever understood myself. In my ignorance, autism was something only boys had, something that was diagnosed in childhood, and the traits were obvious for all to see. I remember there being an autistic boy in our primary school; we were all told of his arrival and how he would behave differently. Looking back,

I remember thinking that his behaviours weren't that weird at all, I was fascinated by him. I think deep down there was burning envy that he was being himself, and there was something beautiful about that.

I was 23 when I finally attended my autism assessment, accompanied by my mum. On our way home I asked her why she and my dad hadn't noticed I was autistic earlier. She softly replied, "We just thought that was you, you were just Hannah." The four pages of double-sided notes on all my childhood oddities, however, said otherwise. My mum had switched from worrying she would not have enough to tell the psychiatrist diagnosing me to suddenly remembering a considerable amount. In a way I am glad that my behaviour was never treated by her as 'disordered' – my friends and the teachers around me had all loved my 'Hannah-isms' – but what I do grieve for is the part of me I had to lose along the way. Sure, if I hadn't hidden so much of my autism then some people might have considered me more of a 'problem', but with that may have come more support and acceptance.

After being diagnosed with Asperger syndrome, a form of autism, I went through many stages of emotions. From the high elation of finally having an answer, of knowing I was not to blame, to the grief and anger that no one had known and helped me sooner. Then followed a sad depression and loss that I did not know who I was and never had, and, finally, a feeling that somewhat resembled acceptance and compassion for myself. But this is not a linear process, and I can regularly jump through all these emotions in a single day, even 10 years later.

Acceptance did not come easily and nor did it come without a lot of work. I have attended therapy every week since I was 22, I have read an awful lot of books (good and not so good), I've cried a lot, I've drawn a lot, and I've had multiple breakdowns. In 2013 I started doing a PhD on the late diagnosis for autistic women so I could begin to answer my own questions, and, more importantly, it gave me the opportunity to talk to a lot of other late-diagnosed autistic adults like myself. It was a journey, and I don't expect that journey will be ending anytime soon; I've got my whole lost childhood and adolescence to make up for! But I am at a point where I feel I've reached the top of the mountain on that journey; I can see everything that came before, and I can see what I need to do next. It's a beautiful, if not slightly daunting, view.

Right now, trying to conceal your autism may be causing you a tremendous amount of pain and conflict. When we camouflage we tell ourselves that the true 'us' is not good enough, that people can't tolerate who we really are, and that we are at fault. But this denies us deeper and more meaningful relationships, not just with others but most importantly with ourselves. So I hope that by reading this book you may gain more insight into your own camouflaging behaviours and begin to notice which ones are helping you, which ones might be hindering you, and how you can start to make small changes to improve your mental wellbeing.

The purpose of this book is to share with you the experiences I have had, the lessons I have learned, and the tools that helped me the most. This isn't about stopping camouflaging altogether; it's about gaining a greater awareness of your thoughts, your beliefs, and your goals. As you will read multiple times in this book, camouflaging isn't necessarily bad: it's a skill all humans adopt and use to grow, and it is how we learned to socialise as a species. In many ways it helped us survive, and for that we should celebrate how clever and incredibly strong we were to learn to do that at such a young age. But here's the thing: just because a strategy we used was once helpful, it doesn't mean it's relevant to our lives now. Sometimes cutting ties with our old habits and behaviours can help us to grow even further. In an ideal world autistic people would be able to access mental health support and work on these things one-to-one with a trained therapist. However, given the lengthy waiting lists many are facing to even be assessed by mental health services, not to mention the expense that private therapy as an alternative can cost, I wanted to publish the tools that helped me most so that they can be made accessible to as many people as possible.

The book is divided into six chapters. The first few start with a gentle introduction into what camouflaging is and what the research says about how we learn it, why we learn it, and what the consequences of using it might be. It is not a complete guide on the topic; for this I would thoroughly recommend *Autism and Masking: How and Why People Do It, and the Impact It Can Have* by Dr Felicity Sedgewick and colleagues (2021). The purpose of this section is really to raise awareness and help to start generating some insights as to how and why you might have been camouflaging. Awareness is really half the solution; once you have this you will be in a far greater position to choose when you want to be camouflaging and when you don't.

The middle chapters are more hands on, with some practical tools and techniques for you to start trying straight away. These tools are made up from commonly used self-help therapeutic methods to explore how you've been camouflaging and how it's been making you feel. Perhaps your diagnosis came out of the blue like mine, and now you're searching for answers as to why it was missed. Perhaps you've been camouflaging for a while and have noticed you've been suffering with depression for a long time too, and now you're asking if they might be linked. Techniques for improving self-esteem and managing anxiety and depression will be explored, for example, methods of learning self-compassion and resetting your beliefs about yourself. Maybe you've been so busy worrying about what everyone thinks of you that nothing feels like it's pleasurable to you any more. Or maybe your self-critical voice has become so loud, while trying to maintain a mask in front of others, that you find you're constantly beating yourself up and worried you'll just make more mistakes. Later chapters in this section will explore ways to practise unmasking yourself in situations where camouflaging hasn't been helpful or might be making you feel bad. For example, perhaps it has been very useful in job interviews but maintaining your mask while at work all day is too exhausting. Perhaps you're having lots of meltdowns and shutting down from your family and friends when you get home from work or school as a result. This part is all about becoming your own advocate, practising to choose when and where you want to camouflage rather than running on social autopilot.

An additional chapter, which can be used by parents, educators, and therapists, is available through JKP Library (see the box at the end of this introduction for specific download instructions). This aims to help explore how an autistic child, pupil, or client may be camouflaging, and what parents, educators, and therapists can do to help them gain more confidence and grow. You might find this resource helpful to share with those around you who are supporting you.

You won't like all the techniques in this book. Some may seem pointless or confusing, or you might totally disagree with them, and that's OK. As a former therapist would frequently tell me, there is no magic wand here. However, what I've tried to do in this book is give plenty of different options and points of view, using my own experience as well as the experience of therapists and other autistic adults throughout. I apologise in advance if you find any of my explanations or exercises patronising. I've tried to write this book for as wide an audience as possible, which means I've included both basic and more complex concepts. Some of this is stuff I wish I'd known as a teenager too, so I've included this for a younger audience. Feel free to take whatever you find useful from the book and then bin the rest.

Through a public call on Twitter I asked for autistic people to come forward and discuss with me over email their experiences of camouflaging and any tactics they might have used to reduce their use of the strategy; their stories and direct quotes from these have been printed throughout the book. Several autism specialist therapists were also consulted; in particular I was lucky enough to receive the support and wisdom throughout of Dr Katharina Hamm, a clinical psychologist who previously worked at the National Adult ADHD and ASD Psychological Service located in the South London and Maudsley NHS Trust, one of very few national mental health services for autism in the UK, which I myself have been fortunate enough to have used. Finally, as I have an academic background in autism as well as personal experience, I've also tried to include key research on the topic throughout. To make sure this is understandable for all readers I have included a glossary of terms used at the beginning of each chapter, and avoided jargon where possible. If you're interested to read more on the studies I have written about, you can use the citations to locate the correct references at the end of the book.

It is perfectly normal when you are working on yourself and exploring parts of your life that have caused you pain that sometimes you might feel worse to start with. If you find this to be too difficult or find you become too distressed, please do seek help from someone who can support you. Details of support lines that can be contacted have been listed in the Disclaimer section at the front of the book. Lastly, there might be things you disagree with in this book too. We all have our own experiences and opinions around autism, but I have tried to use the most commonly used and accepted language, terms, and ideas at the time of writing throughout.

So, in summary, this book is a compilation of my own personal experiences, other autistic voices, psychological research, and self-help materials. I've tried to leave you enough space so that you can complete the exercises in each chapter by writing straight onto the pages of the book. Finally, I wish you all the best with your journey.

Copies of the tables marked ★ and an additional chapter can be downloaded from https://library.jkp.com/redeem using the code KAMDWVM

CHAPTER 1

Learning to Imitate

> ## CHAPTER'S PURPOSE
> To describe how we all develop social bonds with others by learning to imitate those around us, and to normalise the use of camouflaging in autism.

KEY TERMS
- *Camouflaging:* Umbrella term for several behavioural strategies to appear non-autistic
- *Masking:* A form of camouflaging that involves hiding autistic traits
- *Imitation:* Copying the actions and communication used by others
- *Selective mutism:* Severe anxiety that prevents an individual from speaking in certain situations
- *Theory of Mind:* The ability to attribute different mental states to oneself and others
- *Empathy:* The ability to read and share others' feelings

Broadly speaking, camouflaging in autism means using strategies to hide autistic traits to try and fit in with others, and in many ways to appear non-autistic. The research on this is in its infancy, but several studies now have proposed more detailed explanations of the different factors involved in camouflaging. There will be more on this in the next chapter. The idea of camouflaging in autism has become increasing popular over the last few years. For many of us, that first article we read on the topic provided a lightbulb moment that changed everything we knew about autism, and possibly everything we knew about ourselves too. Or, perhaps, for some of you, this book will be your lightbulb moment.

I first learned about camouflaging while reading early books on female autism, in search for answers as to why I had been diagnosed so late, at the age of 23. I had no previous knowledge or awareness that I was autistic, despite finding myself in and out of mental health services unable to find the root cause of my difficulties for many years previously. I needed to know why and how this had been missed. What was it about my autistic traits that meant not a single teacher, psychiatrist, or psychologist throughout my entire life had considered I could be autistic? It wasn't like the signs weren't there. I was a selectively mute and an incredibly anxious child, with severe aversions to textures and foods, eventually dropping out of school at 14 due to the stress the classroom was causing my physical health. But I also performed well at school, had lots of friends, a good sense of humour (depending on who you ask), and all my problems remained bubbling under the surface rather than running riot in outward displays of distress.

I first read Liane Holliday Willey's autobiographical book *Pretending to be Normal* in 2012, a year before my own diagnosis, while I endured the year-long waiting list that is unfortunately all too common for autistic adults. Willey, a Doctor of Education, wasn't diagnosed herself until the age of 35. Since then she has become a passionate author and advocate of diversity and autism awareness. I was struck by how similar our experiences were growing up. She too had found herself watching and mimicking others so much that she had merged their personality into her own (Willey 1999). I realised I'd spent my whole life trying to 'fit in' and trying to be like everyone else. I'd never felt like I was 'normal', and so I'd carefully watched the behaviour of others, from my friends and family to fictional TV and book characters, and gradually adapted my own behaviours to mimic theirs. I'd learned how to give eye contact, tolerating the intense exposure to my eyeballs by counting out the seconds until I could briefly look away. I'd learned how to add intonations into my speech, to move my hands and body to complement the words coming out of my mouth. I learned specific phrases to say, conversation starters, and appropriate facial reactions. Throughout my life my special interest has always been people; I am fascinated with how humans work in the same way that an astronomer is obsessed with understanding how the stars, planets, and universe form and behave.

Thomas did not receive his diagnosis until the age of 59; he described at first being elated to receive this news, but quickly spiralled into a sense of confusion about himself. Rather poignantly he wrote "I quite like the idea of being autistic, but I feel like an imposter." Now 62 and finding himself in yet more therapy, Thomas reflects on how as a child he felt like "The world was a mystery to [him] and [he] did not know what was going on." He comments about his camouflaging, "I feel as though I have been camouflaging as far back as I can remember, but I cannot say that I was trying to 'disguise autistic traits', as I was unaware that I had any autistic traits. I just knew that I felt different, and uncomfortable, and did my best to act in the same way as those around me, so as to not draw attention to myself."

Thomas reflected in his email to me that his main motivation for camouflaging has been to not stand out or be noticed; he believes "if you present yourself as a blank canvas, people will paint whatever they want onto it". Presenting in this way has taken its toll on Thomas greatly. When asked how it made him feel, he described being an intruder, "like [he is] in the living room of a nice family [he] hardly knows. The family are having some kind of social get together, and [he is] being as pleasant as [he] can to fit in, and not upset their evening, but [he] just does not belong there." To cope with the social pressures he began to drink heavily, retreating to his bed with a bottle of vodka by his side.

In my brief email conversations with Thomas, he guided me to a book that had had a significant effect on him when he read it over 30 years ago. Yukio Mishima's Confessions of a Mask *presents the story of a Japanese teenager coming to terms with his sexuality. In the story the main character describes in detail the formation of a false personality that he uses to present himself to the world. Through reading this book, Thomas became more conscious of his own 'mask'.*

For those of us who have been camouflaging for as long as we can remember, it is likely that as children we knew we were different, perhaps even 'alien-like', but that we couldn't put our finger on why. Camouflaging can start as an unconscious strategy, but as we age and learn more we realise what we are doing and how we are doing it. As an adult I am acutely aware of how and when to copy others' behaviour, of when to turn on my camouflaged self. Yes, sometimes it happens automatically before I even realise, but it sits at both a conscious and unconscious level in my mind. Had others not spoken out about their camouflaging, and had I not learned so much about it from others' experiences, I'm not sure I would have ever realised I was doing it too. This is why we have only just entered a new era in our understanding of autism; generations of autistic folk are waking up to the fact that they too have been camouflaging to get by all their lives. As a result, research has begun to explore the consequences of this, but we will discuss this more in Chapter 2.

First, I wanted to begin by discussing how all humans have evolved to want to fit in with those around them socially, and why this has become such an important necessity for us to survive. As an autistic person it is easy to believe that we are 'aliens' compared to our non-autistic cousins, when in actual fact we share many things in common. While our camouflaging strategies may be more ingrained and more resource intensive, it is fair to say that at some time or another every human has learned to mask.

Fitting in to survive

Whether we like it or not, we have been born into this world as part of an incredibly social race of creatures. Our survival as humans has relied on our ability to form bonds with other humans; for our strength as a race lies not in our individual abilities, but in our collective intelligence as a tribe. We do not individually possess the strength of a single lion, however, as a group of humans we can not only prevent that lion from killing each of us, but together we can instead trap and kill an entire pride of lions.

In his book *Sapiens*, describing the history of the human race, Yuval Noah Harari (2014) explains how our ancestors leapt up the food chain through their ability to harness imagination. From this ability to imagine, social constructs were born. We can imagine not only a future point in time where we can gather as a large group with a net and some spears and together outsmart a lion, we can also imagine the relationships with each other within that group. This enhances our ability to successfully work together. For example, I can imagine the attributes that others in a group will want me to have, perhaps strong arms to launch my spears, and also traits which they would deem undesirable, perhaps being too lazy to get up early enough to join them on hunts. I can imagine them gossiping about me when I make a mistake and the shame that would come from that. If I'm disliked then this could result in rejection from my 'tribe', and my ability to survive will be significantly reduced. I cannot defeat a lion on my own.

Why am I rambling on about killing lions in a chapter on camouflaging? Because social camouflaging is not a negative by-product of being autistic; it is an important developmental tool for all humans, born from the need to imitate others and meet others' expectations of us that has been vital for our survival since time began. It might have begun 200,000 years ago, when we still lived in caves and had to hunt in the wild for food, but it is still relevant today. Instead we now face metaphorical lions, for example Twitter trolls or our overly critical bosses. Feeling like we belong to a group of humans, and thus avoiding rejection, is important now more than ever.

We may now be able to survive on our own physically, but our 'old brains', as Professor Paul Gilbert (2009) explains, have not caught up with the times. Our deepest fears as a human are embedded within all of us, whether we are autistic or not. Psychologically, we still feel the pain of being rejected and of that loneliness. And how do we ensure we avoid these fears becoming a reality? We learn to 'fit in' and get along with others. We are constantly socially masking by hiding the aspects of ourselves we think others won't like. However, as I will go on to explain later in this chapter, the level of social camouflaging required for an autistic person to 'fit in' and appear not only non-autistic but also desirable to different groups of people in different contexts takes a ginormous amount more effort. In no small part because of the constant and both subtle, but often times very unsubtle, stigma we face daily. We are too often left to defeat lions alone.

But first, before we can begin to tackle ways of taking off the mask it's important to understand the mechanisms behind it, starting with the first social skill we all learn as infants: the art of imitation.

Monkey see, monkey do

Jean Piaget, a Swiss psychologist born in 1896 who is considered the father of developmental psychology, came up with the idea of 'developmental stages' (Piaget 1972). He noticed while scoring intelligence tests that there were certain mistakes that children always made which adults did not. This demonstrated that humans must learn certain things at certain times in their lives. This included the use of imitation in order to learn how to function symbolically, which is to imagine situations, actions, and others not immediately in front of us. An infant will need to learn to perform certain actions not just in the situation they initially learned them from, but also in new situations too.

But imitation is not just about learning actions, it is also vital for the development of social bonds. Newborns produce positive social connections every time their innate drive to copy other humans' behaviour kicks in (Nadel 2002). With each mimicked tongue protrusion or smile there is a caregiver brimming with pride and love. Without these ties of love and care, babies risk being neglected and left to fend for themselves; the survival of a newborn increases if it is able to evoke strong social feelings in its caregiver.

While an inner drive for all humans to imitate could be present and evidenced from motor mimicking as early as birth

(Meltzoff 2002), much of what we do know about developmental learning is from slightly older infants, those around 18–24 months of age. It is at this point an important feature of imitation develops, the ability to understand how others see us, and from this the beginnings of an understanding of how others' perceptions and beliefs may be different from our own (Meltzoff 1995). The psychological term for this is 'Theory of Mind', although it has been hotly debated for many years in the field of autism. I will discuss this later, but for now it's just important for us to recognise the benefits of this very early developmental stage. For learning this enables us to imagine hypothetical situations, which can be very handy when preparing us for difficult activities, but also somewhat of a curse on those nights when you're up thinking through every possible embarrassing thing you could possibly do!

Developing this perspective-taking skill also better enables us to understand a conversational partner and in doing so creates positive feelings within us (Asendorpf 2002). While for some of us socialising might riddle us with anxiety, many of us will also be able to remember a time when we felt very well connected to the person we were speaking to. For many it is probably when they first met their best friend or partner, finding someone who truly understands and loves you for who you are and with whom you can fully reciprocate those feelings. It can feel like a drug, and indeed each time you successfully 'pull off' a social performance you can feel the buzz and electricity that runs through you and into others around you. A feeling many non-autistic people take for granted and for which autistic people seem to have to fight for, and sadly many of us either have never experienced or do not experience enough.

Last, this development of perspective taking and symbolism leads us straight down the path of developing self-awareness and, most importantly, becoming self-conscious beings (Leith & Baumeister 2008). Embarrassment and shame are unfortunately the primary emotions of this skill. We have learned from imitating others not only how to perform important actions but also who we are and, most importantly, how others see us. Few of us will have never had a flashback to a socially embarrassing situation we feel we messed up in, and then felt that intense shame and cringing that makes you want to physically slap the memory out of your head as violently as possible. For many, the avoidance of this feeling and the perceived social faux pas or 'mess up' is the driving force to wanting to learn how to imitate others and to ensuring one's behaviour is 'socially acceptable' at all costs. Of course, none of this is developed at a conscious level; while individuals may at times become aware they're copying others, it mostly happens 'behind the scenes' in our minds.

Chameleons

Chartrand and Bargh (1999) coined this type of unconscious social imitation the 'Chameleon Effect'. In a series of studies, they found people unconsciously matched their physical behaviours and movements with another person's who they were working on a task with. Following this, they found that when people were being mimicked themselves by another person, it increased their liking of that person. The 'Chameleon Effect' is so strong it has even been observed in studies where participants were tested with a non-human artificial intelligence (AI) partner (Bailenson & Yee 2005). Imitation acts like a social glue, aiding in the development of bonds between people. So deep is our drive to fit in and be liked that people will over-imitate others' pointless actions. Studies have found that when both children and adults are shown how to retrieve a reward from a puzzle box by a demonstrator who performs an obviously irrelevant action, such as tapping the box three times, people will copy this action as well as the necessary actions to retrieve the reward (McGuigan, Makinson, & Whiten 2011). Why? Because people imitate not only to complete an action but also to strengthen the social bond between themselves and others, in this case the experimenter. As we grow our ability to imitate others develops in complexity. Rather than just imitating the use of objects, we copy other people's dress sense, gestures, mannerisms and much more (Carpenter 2006).

Of course, not everyone will do this, and there are varying degrees as to how much different people will imitate others. Chartrand and Bargh (1999) found that those higher in empathy, that is those better able to understand and share the feelings of others, tended to demonstrate the 'Chameleon Effect' to a greater degree. Having a more independent sense of self reduces imitative behaviours too, as the individual does not require the reciprocity of others (van Baaren *et al.* 2003). While being attuned to the social atmosphere increases imitative behaviours, non-autistic adults who employ high levels of self-monitoring in their social surroundings, and are able to adjust their behaviours and ideas according to the social setting, imitate more (Estow, Jamieson, & Yates 2006). Ickes and colleagues (2006) suggested that individuals who self-monitor highly in social situations prefer clearly defined situations so they can use their learned social scripts and plan their behaviour in advance.

Imitation to autistic camouflaging

All the research discussed so far in this chapter is about non-autistic people, but so much of it can be compared to the act of camouflaging in autistic people. The goal is the same: to blend in socially and please those around us. It is often unconscious, although many of us, as we get older, become more aware that we are using the strategy. Also, many of the behaviours are the same: imitating others' dress sense, gestures and mannerisms, and preparing social scripts in advance. Australian psychologist Tony Attwood (2006), describes in his book *The Complete Guide to Asperger's Syndrome* how autistic children often quietly observe what others are doing, going away to practise these behaviours in private before they are confident enough to re-enact them in real social situations; behaviours often mimicked included gestures, tone of voice, and mannerisms. In her book on women and girls on the spectrum, autistic independent autism specialist Sarah Hendrickx (2015) describes how autistic women are like 'little psychologists' as children, and by the time they reach adulthood they have become experts in analysing social behaviour and imitating it.

Rachel was recently diagnosed, and says that part of the reason she camouflages is because she has done so for so long she now

31

finds it difficult to stop. She wrote in her email "It's hard at this point to know where camouflaging ends and my 'real' self begins." I asked her when she feels she first began to camouflage, and like many of the people I spoke to this was impossible for her to pinpoint. However, one particular episode from her childhood sprung out to her. She remembers when she was little "[she] used to walk with [her] hands up in front of [her], at about chest height or maybe waist height, depending. At some point [she] noticed that other people didn't do this, and [she] started consciously trying to stop [herself]."

Rachel's main motivation to camouflage was to "be more like everyone else". She noticed other children making fun of her mannerisms and had struggled to make friends. By imitating those around her she managed to become less of an outsider, though she says that others still considered her "weird". As an adult, Rachel feels a similar pressure to fit in to avoid others thinking she is "weird" or "immature", she wrote in her email, "On one level I believe completely that as autistic people we should be able to express ourselves in the ways that feel comfortable to us, but on another level I'm afraid that people will think less of me if I don't act in expected ways." This fear is particularly relevant to her professional life, where she says she feels that if she doesn't fit in at work then people will think she can't do her job well.

For Rachel, camouflaging provides safety, a way to be less vulnerable around those she doesn't feel deserve her trust. But with that feeling of safety comes exhaustion too, she described feeling "worn out and sort of scattered". She has had to reduce her hours at work because the pressure to wear a mask all day every day became too much. She wrote, "Depending on what exactly the situation is, I sometimes feel as though I have to concentrate quite hard to keep all the plates spinning. Other times, when it's things that come slightly easier and more automatically, it's more like a feeling of holding onto myself too tightly, and often there's a corresponding tension in my actual posture too." Along with this she also feels a great amount of guilt about letting other autistic people down by not being honest about herself, while also *cut off from others who she perceives can be more honest about themselves.*

A long-held myth is that autistic people lack the empathy to understand the perspectives of others. Historically, autism has always been seen as a condition whereby infants lacked social imitation skills and Theory of Mind. This is often part of the reason why many autistic people who camouflage fail to be recognised and receive a diagnosis in childhood. We've all heard the line "but you don't look autistic"; many of us have also been told that we can't possibly be autistic because we understand other people's emotions too well or we have too many friends. But it's long been argued that primary social abilities, such as the ability to imitate, are unaffected by the condition. In a major plot twist for the field newer evidence is even now suggesting autistic people can empathise too much, which hugely calls into question previous theories around the 'normal' development of imitation. In 2014 psychologists Geoffrey Bird and Essi Viding published their model of empathy, which suggested that individuals have a 'self–other' switch that helps regulate shared feelings. It is no good if when we see another person in pain we ourselves are too consumed by sympathy pains to act to help that person. Instead we need to be able to empathise with what that pain must feel like, while switching our minds back to help that person. They suggest that autistic people may struggle to do this more, and so may be so consumed in feeling others' emotions that they have to switch off completely. The theory is much more complex than I can possibly explain within this one chapter, but it certainly helps us to put two fingers up at the myth-driven stigma we often face on the topic.

In an even more interesting twist of events, in 2012 autistic psychologist Damien Milton proposed that rather than autistic people having Theory of Mind and empathy deficits, there is actually a 'double empathy problem' between autistic and non-autistic people. This means that while autistic people may lack the social insights and culture of non-autistic people, non-autistic people too lack the social insights and culture of autistic people. Indeed, it is most probably the case that historically autistic people have actually worked harder to understand non-autistic society than the efforts made by their non-autistic peers. To put it mildly, I've spent at least 30 years of my life studying non-autistic people, I've spent 10 years in therapy, and have undertaken a PhD in psychology to better understand the non-autistic world that surrounds me. Meanwhile, I have struggled to convince several of my previous workplaces to watch an hour-long webinar on how best to work with an autistic person.

While some of this seems a bit off topic, understanding our innate drive to imitate others, and how this develops in both non-autistic and autistic people, is a key part to our understanding of camouflaging. As I've mentioned previously, camouflaging involves the act of mimicking the behaviour of others, but it is also often driven by a deep psychological need to be socially accepted by those around us, fuelled in no small part by a constant stream of uncomfortable self-consciousness.

KEY MESSAGES

- All humans are driven to learn to mimic others' behaviours from a young age, and to fit in with those around them in order to ensure their survival (both physical and psychological).
- This involves both conscious and unconscious intentions and actions.
- Copying others actions and behaviours can act as a 'social glue' that strengthens bonds.
- Feelings of shame and rejection can be the result of not fitting in with others.
- There are many similarities between camouflaging in autism and how all humans learn to imitate others.
- Camouflaging may involve other factors too, and be more ingrained and resource intensive in an autistic person.

CHAPTER 2

The Drive to Camouflage

> **CHAPTER'S PURPOSE**
> To raise awareness of what exactly autistic camouflaging is, who is more likely to camouflage, and what effect it can have.

▨ KEY TERMS

- *Compensation:* A form of camouflaging that involves making up for autistic deficits
- *Phenotype:* An individual's observable traits, such as behaviours
- *Executive functions:* A set of mental skills we use to function
- *Stimming:* Repetitive physical movements that are self-soothing
- *CAT-Q:* Camouflaging Autistic Traits Questionnaire which is used for self-assessing how you camouflage

While the previous chapter attempted to set the scene on camouflaging by explaining how we all develop the ability to imitate others, there is slightly more to autistic camouflaging than imitation alone. While it is fair to say most humans will at some point in their early years learn to copy the behaviours of others, for most this won't affect their lives negatively and will peter out as they pass adolescence. For many of us autistic folk, however, we will still feel the pressure of trying to learn how to adapt in social settings well into adulthood. Studies have shown that the use of camouflaging strategies is much more prominent in autistic people than non-autistic people; it may involve common traits all humans evolve, but it is a strategy embedded in autistic people to a much greater extent (Hull *et al.* 2019).

Dr Wenn Lawson (2020), an autistic expert and advocate in the field, recently published an article which called into question the use of the word 'camouflaging' for this behaviour at all. He says that rather than this term, which suggests a person is purposefully choosing to deceive and put on a 'mask', the term 'adaptive morphing' better captures a behaviour which is often involuntary and vital for keeping an autistic person safe. Many autistic children unconsciously develop strategies to hide their autism in order to protect themselves from others' judgements and bullying, often as a result of previously experiencing negative reactions from others of their autistic traits. Throughout this book I have stuck to the term 'camouflaging', purely because this is the term most commonly used and which most people recognise. However, it is important to remind ourselves that this term does not mean any of us are intentionally setting out to deceive others and I do not wish to minimise our past social trauma.

What is camouflaging?

In 2017 a collaborative study was published that for the first time attempted to identify the key elements of camouflaging (Hull *et al.* 2017). While for many years the community and other autism professionals were aware of camouflaging traits, there were very few published scientific articles to support these experiences. The study interviewed 92 autistic adults on their experiences of camouflaging, and then sought to identify key themes in their responses. Three main themes stood out: (1) motivations for camouflaging, including wanting to fit in and connect with others; (2) the use of strategies, including masking autistic traits, to appear less autistic and compensating for impairments; (3) long- and short-term consequences, including exhaustion and threats to self-identity (more on this later). This has led to the creation of a questionnaire that is simple to use and which reliably measures camouflaging traits in an individual, the Camouflaging Autistic Traits Questionnaire (CAT-Q) (Hull *et al.* 2019). You can take this questionnaire yourself in the next chapter to gain a greater awareness of your own camouflaging.

Naomi self-identified as autistic for many years before being officially diagnosed at the age of 33. They described camouflaging almost constantly, and found this had got worse over the course of their life. When I asked why they camouflaged, they described an "extremely strong need to be liked", embedded within that is an intense fear of being rejected and the depressive feelings this would lead to. They wrote in their email, "It's undeniable that, when I 'act more autistic' i.e. behave more like myself, some people react badly. I have some strong memories of times when this rejection happened, and it has happened many more times that I can't remember. I feel very hopeless about this, because while I want to be myself more (because that's when I'm generally happier), I also don't know if I can handle the rejection and pain that will come with it."

For Naomi camouflaging is a safety net, a protection from the harsh judgements of others. However, this has led to long-term psychological impacts on their self-esteem, and while it has made them feel safer, they are acutely aware that at any moment their mask might slip. They explained how "The moment when it does it feels like the floodgates are opening and shame is pouring in. That horrendous experience of being 'unmasked' can leave [them] sobbing and even wanting to self-injure afterwards."

Just like with autistic traits, camouflaging can also be viewed as a spectrum. Looking at the following table you will see a description of each component of camouflaging from the CAT-Q, and some examples of what those traits can look like more practically. Of course, this is just an example, and you may think of many more which would fit into these categories. You may find some you never do while others you use excessively. Researchers at King's College London, Dr Lucy Livingston and Professor Francesca Happé (2017), described how these different traits may vary greatly in different people. For example, the use of compensation to make up for impairments could be shallow or it could be deep. Some autistic people may struggle to understand the meanings behind jokes, but find it affects them socially not laughing at the correct points. To compensate for this they could either learn to always laugh after a joke, which would be considered shallow compensation, or they might go to great lengths to determine the mechanisms of jokes and understand why they are considered funny and therefore know when they are supposed to laugh, which would be considered deep compensation. It might be that some things you compensate for shallowly, and others deeply, and that these might even vary according to the situation, your mood, and your energy.

For a long time I realised I was simply learning to count out my eye contact with people to compensate for struggling to maintain eye contact in social situations. This would be defined as 'shallow compensation', as I wasn't really finding an alternative route to overcome this difficulty, I was covering my tracks. But sometimes there just isn't a deeper route, we can't make ourselves become something we aren't, and in many ways I found it easier to concentrate and respond appropriately in conversations without the burden of eye contact. On the other hand, I've spent years unconsciously figuring out the different types of intentions and emotions behind what people say and the expressions on their faces, how these can match up and how they may change in different contexts. This would be considered a deeper type of compensation. I've not just learned what emotion goes with each facial expression and the correct way to respond to this, I've learned that expressions and emotions can be more nuanced and therefore I'm less likely to make a mistake in my interpretations and subsequent reactions. Notice how formulaic this is beginning to all sound? At some point we might take on these characteristics more naturally, but how exhausting it is to have to learn and practise them constantly for every social situation we encounter.

Camouflaging traits and descriptions

Trait	Description	Examples
Masking	Hiding autistic traits to appear non-autistic	Monitoring facial expression, eye contact, body posture, and voice intonation during an interaction, e.g. ensuring your voice isn't flat and that you seem interested in the other person, that you aren't looking at something else and that you are behaving similarly to them.
		Having special interests that are deemed 'socially acceptable', e.g. obsessing over a popular celebrity or playing a popular game that you know your peers like too.
		Suppressing stims in public, e.g. clasping your hands tightly so you don't flap them when excited or rub them together over and over.
Compensation	Compensating for autistic traits that make socialising more difficult	Learning how to behave in social situations by watching how someone else behaves, e.g. closely watching a friend, a celebrity on TV, or character from a book to gauge how they act in certain situations.
		Mentally practising social situations before engaging in them, e.g. imagining made-up scenarios in your head (or in front of a mirror) and how you would act and respond.
		Learning a social script of what to say in certain situations, e.g. greeting people with a specific learned phrase such as 'Hi, how're you?'
		Researching how specific social situations are supposed to go, e.g. learning specific rules for different social contexts, such as when to not overshare.

cont.

Trait	Description	Examples
Assimilation	Trying to fit in with others	Feeling that you have to put an effort in to interact with others, e.g. you don't often want to interact with others but you feel you have to, and that it doesn't come naturally to do so.
		Feeling like you are performing when you interact with others, e.g. you can't really be yourself, the conversation isn't natural, and you find you need to practise a social script.
		Feeling that you need support to socialise, e.g. you need to have your friend or partner by your side and you need their reassurance throughout.

Camouflaging is a balancing act that takes years of practise and trial and error, without us even realising we are doing it. We didn't all wake up one morning when we were four and decide that we might get along better with our friends if we flapped our hands less and copied their facial expressions more. Having said that, and after reading this book, you will have probably become acutely more aware of these camouflaging behaviours, and that's OK. Part of gaining the control back is knowing yourself better and considering the situations in which camouflaging may and may not be helping you.

Why do autistic people camouflage?

There is no single reason as to why some autistic people camouflage, however research points to a number of different abilities, skills, and attributes that might aid camouflaging. Additionally, a number of social factors may act as a catalyst. You can see some of these in Figure 2.1; colour in any that you think be true for you.

Gender

Initially the concept of camouflaging in autism was thought to be a *female phenotype* of autism spectrum condition (ASC) (Kopp & Gillberg 1992), meaning that autistic girls and women display their traits differently to the typical display seen in boys and men. That's not to say the core traits were different, just how they appeared. For example, girls internalise a lot of their struggles, often becoming anxious and mute, whereas boys externalise their struggles, often becoming more hyperactive and vocal (Solomon *et al.* 2012). When it comes to repetitive and restricted behaviours, boys tend to display more of these compared to girls too (Mandy *et al.* 2012), meaning that for teachers, parents, and clinicians, the signs of autism are much easier to observe in boys than girls. Indeed, this is considered one of the leading theories as to why for many girls their diagnoses don't come until adulthood (Baldwin and Costley 2016).

Figure 2.1 Factors contributing to camouflaging

Part of this theory is that females demonstrate fewer external autistic traits because they are *camouflaging*. When looking at scores on the CAT-Q (Camouflaging Autistic Traits Questionnaire) this does seem to be the case. In Hull and colleagues' (2020) assessment of this measure, females scored on average 124 out of a total 175 points compared to males who scored on average 110 out of 175 points (non-autistic females scored 91 and non-autistic males scored 97 on average). In school-aged children some studies have found that girls exhibit better friendships with other children than autistic boys (Sedgewick *et al.* 2016) and more engagement in joint activities with other children than autistic boys too (Dean, Harwood, & Kasari 2017), both suggesting the use of camouflaging by the girls to enhance their social performances.

But why would girls use camouflaging more in the first place? Some people think that females may be born with better mental abilities that aid camouflaging; some of these will be discussed in more detail next, but this may include better memory of social scripts and more inhibition of 'undesirable' behaviours (Livingston *et al.* 2018). The other major reason that may explain enhanced camouflaging for autistic females is how boys and girls are socialised from birth. Society dictates our gender norms; these are sets of rules about what society believes is 'masculine' and what is 'feminine'. The gender norms in Western cultures have historically stereotyped males as being aggressive, dominant, and independent, among other traits. In contrast, females have typically been stereotyped as being gentle, sympathetic, shy, sensitive to others' needs, and compassionate, among other traits (Bem 1981). Although the feminist movement has meant society is becoming more aware of this possible social construct of gender, it still remains ingrained in much of our society (Fine 2010). Therefore it is likely that just as the general population experiences social learning of gender norms that affect behaviour, autistic boys and autistic girls also experience this, shaping how their autistic traits manifest at a behavioural level. This may mean that autistic females are motivated to fit in more socially and to be quieter and more empathic towards others. It is also highly likely that parents exert this pressure onto their daughters, pushing them to behave in ways considered socially acceptable for their gender. How many times as children did us girls experience being told to 'be more ladylike' whenever we became too boisterous while playing, talked over others too loudly, obliviously sat with our legs apart, or preferred wearing looser, more comfortable clothing? I remember the pain as a child of being forced to attend school friends' birthday parties wearing an itchy frock and tights I couldn't stand; I would proceed to cry until someone either took me home or let me change into some comfier 'boy' clothing. Even as an adult my wardrobe is split into clothing I enjoy wearing – joggers, jeans, baggy tees, and hoodies – and clothing I've selected precisely for the purpose of 'going out' and fitting in as a female – a couple of dresses, fitted trousers, and blouses. Incidentally, I only seem to get compliments when wearing the latter, despite feeling so far removed from my true self whenever I'm out in that girly gear.

However, and this is a big however, research on autism has historically oversimplified and divided gender. Sometimes this is for good reason; research resources can be limited and it's more difficult to find large enough numbers of autistic individuals identifying as other genders like non-binary. But there is no excuse for continuing to perpetuate this idea that there is a male brain and female brain, and specific behaviours and abilities can be attributed to one or the other. In reality this simply isn't the case. Just as how previously autism was considered a 'male disorder' representing an extreme form of the male mind (Baron-Cohen 2012), we now know that there's also a fair few more autistic females than we thought hiding in plain sight! We also know that some girls like things we'd consider 'boyish' and some boys like things considered 'girlish'.

The numbers from the research may show that on *average* autistic girls and women camouflage more, but this summary ignores the many autistic boys and men who also camouflage. No research states that camouflaging is exclusively used by females, in fact Hull and colleagues (2020) found that the average male camouflaging scores were higher than the non-autistic general population's, and higher still for non-binary autistics (although this sample was rather small). When looking at specific items on the questionnaire there were no differences between males and females for how much they compensated for autistic deficits either, only in their levels of masking and desire to fit in with others. Indeed, some recent studies suggest that the difference in camouflaging lies not in how much males and females attempt to camouflage, but rather in the quality of it. Cassidy and colleagues (2018) found that 89 per cent of autistic women and 91 per cent of autistic men in their sample attempted to camouflage, yet the women seemed to camouflage in more places, more often, and for longer.

What we know thus far about camouflaging is based on the female experience of it. I've included being female here as a factor that might increase camouflaging, but as you can see it's more complicated than this, and other factors come into play too. There is growing evidence that some autistic girls do face different challenges and social experiences in childhood than autistic males, which may create an environment around an autistic girl that encourages camouflaging. But much more research is needed in this area that's inclusive of *all* genders, before any such conclusions are made.

Functioning, abilities, and skills

Camouflaging isn't one behaviour; we aren't born with a button that once pressed immediately disguises our autism. Instead it's a collection of many different traits and behaviours, as we saw earlier in this chapter from those researchers who have examined the factors that make up camouflaging, that take effort and different skills. Some people might use one of those strategies, while others might use many. In order to be able to use these strategies we need to have developed certain skills and abilities that make them possible to use. We can't mimic others' behaviour unless we have the ability to remember the behaviour we have seen. We can't apply our learned social scripts to new situations without the ability to plan ahead and be flexible to new situations and changes. Similarly, we can't hide our stimming behaviours, like hand flapping and finger tapping, unless we are able to inhibit and supress our automatic movements. These kinds of skills are referred to as 'executive functions'; they are skills that involve mental process to control our behaviours and actions. Executive functions include attention, inhibition, memory, flexibility, planning, reasoning, and problem solving.

What does executive functioning look like in the real world?

I'll take an example from my own daily life to try and illustrate what this can look like. I'll admit, it takes me quite a long time to get out of bed and get ready in the morning, and it also takes me a really long time to get ready for bed at night. I put both tasks off with an almost professional level of procrastination. Sometimes I need prompting to do this, or help to get things ready, and even then I can find myself over an hour behind my planned schedule. While some of this is down to my need to stick to the same 'getting ready' routine, a big part of this problem is the difficulties I experience in planning and executing a plan that has multiple activities. I need to choose and prioritise what I need to do; this involves multitasking different actions and planning ahead. I also need to remember what I was doing and what I need to do next. Often this leads to a complete overwhelm in my head about what should be a very simple and common set of tasks. I do this every day of my life, and yet it remains a struggle. However, on the flip side of this I have a very good memory of past events, what people said, what they were wearing, and where we were. This helps me immensely when it comes to mimicking how others have behaved in specific social interactions and situations.

In 1996 American psychologists Professors Bruce Pennington and Sally Ozonoff conducted a lengthy review on research articles concerning problems in executive functioning, concluding that they're significantly more likely to occur in autistic people and those with attention deficit hyperactivity disorder (ADHD) (Pennington & Ozonoff 1996). Since this executive functioning theory of autism came about, it has been backed up by a steady stream of research (Otterman *et al.* 2019).

This raises the question, if camouflaging involves executive functioning, and autistic people have poorer executive functioning skills, how has camouflaging become a strategy used by autistic people at all? This might partially explain why camouflaging is so exhausting. How often do you return home from what others deem a 'minor' social interaction only to find yourself conked out for the rest of the day and possibly even the next? As an adolescent I could only schedule one social event a week because I knew it would take me the rest of the week just to recover. Livingston and colleagues (2018) explained how camouflaging uses up valuable resources, which could otherwise be used elsewhere. Indeed, in studies that have interviewed autistic people about their camouflaging, many reported severe emotional consequences, including exhaustion (Hull *et al.* 2017; Tierney, Burns, & Kilbey 2016). While all humans, both autistic and non-autistic, may wear a mask in different social situations, the internal resources required to do this are much greater for autistic people and take a far greater toll.

There may also be differences between autistic individuals in what executive functioning difficulties are present. While some may find they have poor memory, others may find they have a fantastic, almost photographic, memory. It is once again a spectrum of skills and deficits at play. Recent studies have found that better executive functioning seems to be associated with more camouflaging traits. In particular, those who score highly on measures of executive functioning seem to demonstrate higher abilities to compensate for their autistic deficits, which hopefully you will remember from earlier in this chapter is a key factor in camouflaging (Hull *et al.* 2017; Livingston *et al.* 2018).

The role of executive functions may also help partially explain the gender differences we see in camouflaging use. Several studies have shown that autistic females have fewer problems with executive functioning than autistic males do (Bolte *et al.* 2011; Lai *et al.* 2012). Why this is, we do not know. The reasons may lie in the physical differences observed between male and female brains, for example camouflaging has been found to correlate positively with cerebellum grey matter for autistic women (Lai *et al.* 2017). This next bit is a bit technical, so don't worry if neuroscience isn't your specialist subject. The cerebellum sits at the back of our heads and is covered by both grey and white matter. This grey matter contains most of our neuronal cell bodies, and is key in communication across the brain. This area of the cerebellum in particular has been shown to play an important role in executive functions such as learning, memory, multitasking, and inhibition (Bellebaum & Daum 2007).

While specific mental abilities and skills appear to help us camouflage, we can only really guess how and why. We still have no idea what causes which – for example, while executive functions may help us camouflage, so too might camouflaging help us practise and better our executive functions. We have no way of knowing what comes first, but our brains are extremely flexible and are able to develop and learn new things all the time. There's no reason why, over time, an autistic person with poor executive functioning might not find a way to compensate for these executive difficulties using other brain functions, and so be able to camouflage despite these problems. I may be terrible at getting myself ready in the morning and for bed at night, but I've developed coping mechanisms that mean I really thrive in a job where I'm responsible for planning a project. I make numerous lists, set reminders, break down each task into much smaller components, and provide myself and others with weekly summaries of what's been done and what needs doing the following week. A particular strength that lots of autistic people have is the ability to systemise (Baron-Cohen *et al.* 2003), that is to understand how to analyse and construct systems, and so it is that I find life much easier when I can turn the abstract and vagueness into its own system.

Being different and facing stigma

We turn now to our last main factor, a key social motivation for camouflaging: being different. Being autistic makes you different in a variety of ways to the rest of the non-autistic population, and that difference goes to the very core of our social existence as humans. If we consider the intolerance many people have for the small differences and variations even within their own section of society, then it is no wonder autistic people face the levels of stigma and bullying that they so often sadly do. While in his book, *The Presentation of Self in Everyday Life* (1990), American sociologist Erving Goffman discussed how all humans navigate social situations as a stage to perform appropriately in front of others and to avoid shame, it is fair to surmise that this so-called 'stage' is about quadruple the size for autistic people and surrounded by hot lava. Perhaps, as autistic people, we should instead of a stage think of social interactions like the game 'The Floor is Lava', whereby we are constantly required to jump out of our comfort zones to meet the social requirements of others, risking life and limb as we go. If performing appropriately in different social situations is like learning to ride a bike for non-autistic people, for us it's like learning to ride a bike up a hill while the ground is on fire. The need to avoid shame and stigma because of our different social presentation therefore runs much deeper. Goffman (1990) describes how we all need a 'back stage' where we can relax and don't have an audience; however, the issue is that for some even this 'back stage' requires a performance. This might just be the crux to why autistic camouflaging is much more exhausting than non-autistic social performing; there is no 'back stage', our whole lives are affected by keeping up a non-autistic performance.

My greatest fear in life has always been of embarrassing myself or others seeing me 'out of control'. By out of control I mean acting in a way that lets slip my social 'performance', such as being ill in front of others, having a panic attack, crying, getting angry, or even just saying something that's a bit odd. If someone informs me, or insinuates, that what I've said or done has upset them or is inappropriate in some way, I feel myself internally crippled over with embarrassment and shame. It is absolutely intolerable, and I still have flashbacks from years and years ago of very minor things I did or said that weren't appropriate or just seemed weird. Living with this fear and the social differences that come with autism is traumatic. It is no wonder that we develop a reaction to avoid that trauma; if we camouflage ourselves and avoid these mishaps and faux pas then we avoid that crippling shame too. Studies have found that approximately 29 per cent of autistic people reach clinical levels for social anxiety disorder (Hollocks *et al.* 2019), meaning that quite a number of autistic people aren't just shy in social situations but acutely fear them.

This fear isn't unjust. In 2002 a research article was published stating that 94 per cent of mothers reported that their autistic child had experienced peer victimisation (Little 2002). Other studies have reported much lower levels of bullying experienced by autistic children than these earlier figures, but these numbers are still considered concerning (van Roekel, Scholte, & Didden 2010). It's true that most children will have memories of being ostracised or left out by their peers, but far fewer will have experienced the same constant rejection and abuse that autistic children face daily as a result of their social differences. This discrimination isn't just experienced in childhood either: the National Autistic Society (NAS 2016) published results from a survey of over 2000 autistic adults, which said that 48 per cent of respondents had experienced bullying or harassment in the work place.

Ketsia realised she was autistic at the age of 36, although she hasn't had an official diagnosis. She described her camouflaging as "an active suppression of certain behaviours that were seen as odd or disturbing to others". In the email she wrote to me she told me how she has expressed her true self and needs, only to have people look at her with "disgust, fear or expressed annoyance". She wrote how "mortifying" and "ashamed" she felt about herself after these interactions. She writes: "Every time this has happened, I have learned to never do this in public again, watch my tongue and keep more and more things to myself." The fear of drawing negative attention to herself or being seen as a "pariah" has been the driving force behind Ketsia's use of camouflaging.

When I asked how this made her feel, she said, "Exhausted." She described needing long amounts of time afterwards to recharge. Tied in with this was the feeling that she was living her whole life as a performance, and losing her identity. She wrote, "I think I spend a good deal of my waking life camouflaging, and I have come to feel as if life is a chore, a duty; there is no pleasure in it. It has led to anhedonia. Camouflaging is being selfless in a way because you are focused on what people expect of you and you are entirely living to please others. If you spend too much time in that mode, you will end up feeling bitter at people, especially those who ask too much of you."

I was never aware as a child that I was being viewed differently, and neither did I experience the severe victimisation and bullying that so many other autistic children do. But I do vividly remember many situations in which I was made to feel 'weird' and 'wrong' for the way I was. In one of these scenarios I had been invited to a sleepover in secondary school by a girl who didn't particularly like me. I'm not sure why the invite was extended at all, but I think it had something to do with her wanting to recruit my best friend at the time into her friendship group. My best friend was much cooler and prettier than I was, and one's ability to get boys' attention had started to become a valuable currency, a currency in which my net worth was estimated to be in negative figures. I was aware that I only really knew and felt comfortable with one other girl at this sleepover, my best friend, and it quickly became apparent that I was to be the focus of ridicule that evening. I had carefully picked out my pyjamas with my mum before the sleepover; where usually I'd wear boyish, baggy pyjama bottoms and a t-shirt, I felt I needed to wear something different to fit in with this group of popular 'girly' girls. So we decided on a cute Marks and Spencer's, pink and white check nightdress. Of course, this wasn't particularly cool for a 13-year-old girl, and my failed attempts to mask myself while wearing this nightdress had made them laugh at me even more.

Recently, research has turned to measuring how non-autistic people perceive the social behaviours of autistic people who they don't know are autistic, to determine levels of prejudice associated with the condition. Dr Noah Sasson and colleagues (2017), from the University of Texas, showed short video clips of autistic people performing a mock audition for a reality/game show to a group of non-autistic peers. These peers were asked to rate these videos, as well as the videos of non-autistic people doing the same audition, on a first impressions scale. What they found was troubling. Despite not knowing which participants were autistic, the videos of autistic people were rated as being more socially awkward, and less attractive and likeable. Participants also expressed that they were less likely to hang out with, sit next to, or talk to the autistic participants, based purely on watching and listening to 10 seconds' worth of their performances. I wanted to find out how much camouflaging affected these first impressions. Do autistic people who score more favourably use camouflaging more to hide their autistic traits? This was a hard question to ask; it's hard enough to find scientific evidence that your diagnosis makes others see you as less, but harder still to find out that trying to be somebody else to the detriment of your own wellbeing somehow improves your likeability. It was also an important question to ask though – not to find out if we should be encouraging autistic people to camouflage more so they face less stigma and discrimination, but so we can begin to raise awareness among non-autistic people of their unconscious biases, and begin to change society to accept these differences. In our study we found no evidence that higher self-ratings of camouflaging by autistic people led to more favourable first impressions, but we did find that females and those diagnosed with autism later seemed to be rated more highly by peers (Belcher *et al.* 2021). This might suggest that while intent to camouflage doesn't change how we are viewed by others, other mechanisms are at play that do, such as the quality and depth of that camouflaging.

These studies tell us that there is a bias in how autistic behaviour is viewed – one that might drive an autistic person to cover those traits and behaviours in order to be accepted. But what it does not show is the reverse, that is, how do autistic people view non-autistic people, and likewise how do autistic people view other autistic people? As mentioned in the previous chapter, there is likely a double empathy problem here. Both autistic and non-autistic people lack the same social norms that the other deems important, it is not that autistic people just generally lack social skills at all. It might be easier to think of them instead as two different cultures. Morrison and colleagues (2020) found that while autistic people did rate other autistic people's behaviours as less favourable than non-autistics', these ratings didn't affect their social interest for interacting with these people in the same way it did for non-autistic people. Furthermore, several studies have now found that when non-autistic people are told the individuals they are rating are autistic, it improves their ratings (Sasson & Morrison 2019). It seems with more awareness comes greater empathy. Historically, autistic people have been taught to change themselves to fit in with others, and camouflaging fits in with this dialogue that it is the autistic person at fault and who needs to adapt. Of course there are times where it is important for us to adapt, when an autistic child has very challenging and quite harmful behaviours, or when social skills are indeed severely impacted, but what if on the whole we instead focused on teaching society tolerance and more acceptance for human variance? Would this not benefit us all?

In his book *Neurotribes* (2017) award-winning American author Steve Silberman echoes this not-so-radical idea, that society could afford to be a little more tolerant and accepting. However, he goes on to explain how realistically it is not, and that historically it has been easier to change an individual's behaviour than it has the whole of society's. In a talk delivered at Durham University, on social disability in autism, Dr Noah Sasson (2021) stated that 'the solution is not to normalise the autistic person, but to understand the behaviour and adjust for it'. While this may be quite a tall order, it doesn't mean we should abandon hope. If each of us individually chose to be a little more like our real selves every day, educating those around us, then gradually we could turn the tide. But this takes an awful lot of bravery and energy.

I never felt more at home than when I made my first autistic friend. While I value all my non-autistic friendships a great deal and they all accept me and love me for exactly who I am, my autistic friends produce a very different type of bond. There is no stigma here, no fear of saying or doing the wrong thing, and a mutual understanding and appreciation for each other's strengths and weaknesses. I can be the same person I am at home hanging out with my cats that I can be around these people. Despite our supposed 'social skill deficit' I have had far fewer social mishaps and faux pas with these people; we communicate directly but not devoid of emotion or empathy. I liken this bond to the feeling you get when you fall in love with someone. The puzzle pieces from each of you fall into place together and there is an electricity in that which excites you both. It was not until I made my first proper autistic friend that I realised what I had been missing by trying to fit into this uninhabitable alien world of 'neurotypical'. I realised that social interactions weren't supposed to be this exhausting and difficult, that I too could have that fluidity of socialising that I never thought attainable. We can monologue to each other about our special interests without any rebuke that we are talking too much or repeating ourselves. There is no assumption that a lack of eye contact means we are disinterested or not engaged, in fact it often means the opposite. We don't have to move our faces to express ourselves, or make small talk about the weather and each other's days before every conversation. Most of our conversations don't begin with a 'Hi, how're you?' but instead a 'Did you know...' or 'I feel rubbish today...', whatever we actually want to talk about. And yet despite an absence of all the behaviours we assume are vital for social interaction, the interaction still works. In her book *Somebody Somewhere* (1998) Australian writer, singer-songwriter, screen writer, and sculptor Donna Williams wrote about how to feel 'normal' we just need to be in the company of people like ourselves.

From the day we are born we are taught what it means to be 'us'. We are taught how to behave according to our gender and to society's norms. If this doesn't match who we really are then we begin our lives pretending to be someone we are not. So far in this chapter we have explored several reasons as to why someone might camouflage, and you will see that there is no single reason, but rather lots of mixed and interacting factors, at a biological level, cognitive level, and social level too. Many people have long thought camouflaging was a distinctively female autistic strategy, but instead it seems that being female is just one extra factor that can accentuate that drive to conform and 'fit in'. It is one layer of an onion that has many other layers; the more layers you add the more likely you are to have learned to camouflage and the deeper it goes. Part of this journey is to figure out what makes you, you. What has your camouflaging been hiding and how has it been making you feel? In order to do that we need to understand our pasts and the factors that have contributed to how we've learned to behave. The effects these factors may have had on us will be explored next.

The effects of camouflaging

When I was 14 I became too physically unwell to go to school daily. It started with every other week off until gradually I couldn't attend at all. At the time the doctors could not place what was wrong with me; I was experiencing a mixture of stomach problems, menstrual problems, and a great deal of anxiety. Many told me I was skiving and needed to force myself to go in. Eventually, when I got to college I started to try and attend, although I managed on average about 15 per cent of my classes. When I did go in I was often too fatigued to participate, spending half my days sitting in the toilet cubicle blocks or collapsed on a table in the canteen away from other students. As I grew older and overcame my agoraphobia, leaving the house more and more and learning to deal with my physical symptoms outside the house, I noticed I'd still have these periods of excessive fatigue. For several months I would manically rush around from social event to social event, trying to make up for lost time, before descending into a state of anxiety, depression, and despair that would too often land me in the A&E department threatening to take my own life. Before an autism diagnosis was even considered I had gathered several alternative diagnoses, including major depression, generalised anxiety disorder, and bipolar II. It occurred to me that the reason for these crashes was because those months I was manically socialising exhausted me. I couldn't bear a simple conversation and the slightest change or upset would send me into a meltdown. If I ever wanted to overcome these mental health difficulties I'd need to pace myself better, ensuring I paid better attention to my warning signs, and have regular breaks away from environments that caused me to camouflage. Interestingly, the period of time in 2020 that we all spent in some form of lockdown as a result of the Covid-19 virus highlighted to me how detrimental the way I had been socialising was to my mental health. I found myself for the first time ever in my life completely devoid of the constant anxiety I had been experiencing daily. I found myself more able to concentrate on my work, without using the little resources I had to 'fit in' with my work colleagues and with the complete strangers I had to endure the 40-minute commute with to and from work. In a study I have been involved with, led by colleagues at University College London, we explored the effects of Covid-19 on the mental health of autistic people. While there was a long list of reasons for worsening mental health among these participants during this time, it became apparent that many autistic people were also feeling like there'd been a weight lifted off their shoulders; they weren't having to go out and therefore weren't having to camouflage as much, which had eased some of their anxiety (Bundy *et al.* 2021). While in my own therapy, looking at my use of camouflaging, I drew the vicious cycle in Figure 2.2 that I found myself perpetually stuck in:

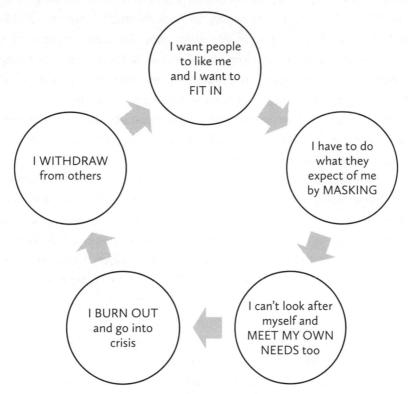

Figure 2.2 Cycle of camouflaging

The research is pretty clear that camouflaging can and does affect mental health. The higher autistic people score on the CAT-Q for camouflaging the worse they score for traits of anxiety and depression (Hull *et al.* 2019). Even more concerning is the strong association found between camouflaging and suicidal behaviours. Dr Sarah Cassidy, from the University of Nottingham, has carried out a number of survey-based studies which demonstrate that camouflaging is a significant predictor of suicidal behaviours in autistic people (Cassidy *et al.* 2018). Additionally, higher levels of thwarted belonging – when the need to connect to other people is unmet – are also related to higher levels of suicidality (Pelton & Cassidy 2017). Sure, there could be a third factor at play here: perhaps some of the reasons that prompt camouflaging to develop in early childhood and lead to thwarted belonging could also cause anxiety and depression in later life too, such as being bullied or ostracised, for example. However, in Cassidy and colleagues' (2018) initial study they controlled for differences in their subjects' age, sex, developmental condition, employment, satisfaction with living arrangements, *and* traits of depression and anxiety, meaning that high camouflaging traits alone were able to predict higher levels of suicidal behaviours even without any of these possible third factors contributing. So what exactly is it about camouflaging that can have such a severe impact on our mental health?

There are two key possibilities here: one is that camouflaging can be mentally quite exhausting, and another is the deeper effects hiding one's true self can have on self-esteem and feelings of our identity. As I mentioned previously, some of the mental skills necessary, such as memorising social scripts and inhibiting responses, can be mentally draining, especially if you find that you're around others and camouflaging most of your day. Livingston and colleagues (2018) suggested that some of these resources being used to camouflage mean they can't be used elsewhere. For example, while away at university I really struggled on my course to achieve the kind of top grades I was used to getting when I was socially isolated at school and college. I became academically distinctly average, and sometimes worse than average. The problem was that because I was living in shared houses with lots of other students I was constantly having to camouflage – from 9am when I got up and had breakfast in the shared kitchen to 2am when the other students seemed to finally head to bed and I could have some time to myself again.

Even though lots of these people became good friends, I still couldn't be 100 per cent relaxed and my full autistic self. This left no energy or resources to put towards studying. You may find the same thing happens to you all day at work, or even at home if you live in a hectic household.

Authenticity and the loss of identity is a slightly trickier problem to interpret. We are a minority group, albeit actually now quite a large one (Solomon 2014). Like any minority group we have fought throughout history to claim our identity and find our self-worth. In 2007 Dr Nancy Bagatell, from the University of North Carolina, published an interesting case study on an autistic young man called Ben and his process of identity construction. As a young man Ben was increasingly exposed to social skills training and therapy that encouraged him to 'fit in' but, rather than helping him become less lonely, he became more and more depressed. He felt that he was failing at being 'normal', and Bagatell (2007) explains how this framework of what is 'normal' has been constructed outside of the autistic experience and had led to the oppression of Ben's natural behaviours. After being exposed to other autistic people, whom he learned were also trying to fit in and become 'normal', he started to see autism as part of his identity, something that couldn't be separated or hidden from his personality. We cannot be our authentic selves if we are oppressing and denying such a massive part of ourselves. That doesn't mean necessarily denying it is a disability, although some choose to; it's about understanding who we really are and what we really like, without the constraints of what society expects of us. To live in opposition to our 'true self' is quite frankly soul destroying. To deny ourselves the activities we like to do and the 'special interests' we want to partake in all in the name of seeming more 'normal' to others, is denying us of our right to enjoy our lives. Ben learned through his newfound community an understanding of himself that he could have a meaningful life as an autistic person, not in spite of his autism.

Ellen was diagnosed at the age of 27. Like many other undiag-nosed autistic children she was aware that she was having to control herself to fit into certain situations, but did not realise this was linked to autism. Once she started to learn more about her autism, she made some candid observations about her attempts to camouflage; she writes in her email, "I was struggling with my authentic self who wanted to be honest and open, and the belief that I had to try and act like everyone else and hide my true self, which was clamouring to be out in the open and accepted by others." Ellen describes much of her camouflaging as happening automatically; she comments, "My 'mask' feels like part of me too and I don't always know what is camouflaging and what is not." She is stuck between her drive to conform to be accepted and her longing to be more authentic and create her own boundaries, describing how this inner conflict has made her feel quite "discombobulated".

She also describes the loneliness of not being able to share her inner experiences, and a sense of uncertainty at constantly having to predict how others will react to her social interactions. One of the main consequences to her camouflaging has been great amounts of fatigue, from having to constantly work overtime during conversations to maintain her mask. In her email she describes consciousness as having a "bottle neck", "[she is] aware that [hers] is at full capacity. In contrast, when [she] feels comfortable to drop [her] mask, [she] has so much more mental energy for keeping track of the conversation and thinking curiously and creatively."

While autistic people are much more vulnerable to anxiety and depression than the rest of the population, the more positive their own autistic identity is the better their self-esteem has been found to be (Cooper, Smith, & Russell 2017). In their article, appropriately titled 'Putting on My Best Normal', Hull and colleagues (2017) found that almost 60 per cent of their autistic participants said that they did not feel like their true selves because of camouflaging. They felt increasingly isolated around others, one commenting "I feel sad because I feel like I haven't really related to the other people. It becomes very isolating because even when I'm with other people I feel like I'm just playing a part." Others felt they lost who they really were, one participant commenting, "Sometimes, when I have had to do a lot of camouflaging in a high stress environment, I feel as though I've lost track of who I really am, and that my actual self is floating somewhere above me like a balloon." Goffman (1900) too warned that if one's social performance is not one that is authentic to the person, and may be even at conflict with one's 'true self', then this would lead to alienation.

When I started at university I got rid of all the things that were associated with my autistic self. I didn't know I was autistic at the time, but I knew they wouldn't be considered 'normal' by my peers and I needed to mask this part of me. I put aside the silky bear I'd had since a child, whose material I found soothing to repeatedly scratch and rub against my lip. I stopped watching the kids shows I found entertaining, in case someone nearby would overhear me, and I stopped collecting and putting on display the random items and objects I picked up daily that I treasured. Instead I plastered my large pinboard with images and posters I thought would make others think I was 'cool'. After the years went by of me continually oppressing my interests and habits I forgot who I was and what I enjoyed. I began to feel empty and depressed. Was I even a real person? Nothing brought me joy and I felt I'd just become a robotic clone of what people wanted me to be. Part of my recovery from this mental health crisis was relearning what made me happy again. I surrounded myself with all the things I knew I once liked, the toys, the games, TV programmes, clothing, and music. It wasn't easy, publicly expressing my true self was quite frankly terrifying at times, but it worked. I still feel a sense of shame around enjoying these things and hide it as much as I can from more formal settings, like work, but having these things to look forward to and surround myself with in my home life has saved me from many further meltdowns and mental health crises. Part of my recovery was learning to do activities that had no other purpose to them other than for enjoyment's sake. As one autistic friend once said to me, "We are human beings, not human doings".

Hopefully this chapter has given you a whistle stop tour into what exactly camouflaging is, what scientists have discovered about it, and how it might be affecting your life. The ultimate question is, is camouflaging worth the effort? This is up to you to decide for yourself. At what expense to both your identity and your energy is camouflaging? Are you getting back from society the same effort you're putting in? In the next part of this book we explore a little more about when and how you've been camouflaging, how it's been affecting you, and what it might be like if you reduced these behaviours.

◼ KEY MESSAGES

- Camouflaging involves several factors, including masking, compensation, and assimilation.
- Some factors that make a person more likely to camouflage include being autistic, being brought up female, having good executive functions, and experiencing social stigma.
- Studies have shown that camouflaging has a significant negative effect on mental health, possibly due to the exhaustion of constantly using the strategy and also the loss of one's true self.

CHAPTER 3

Do You Camouflage?

> ### CHAPTER'S PURPOSE
> To explore whether you are currently using
> any camouflaging strategies and the type of
> settings you use these most in and why.

KEY TERMS
- *CBT:* Cognitive behavioural therapy, which is used for managing thoughts, feelings, and behaviours
- *Alexithymia:* Difficulties reading and understanding one's own emotions

The purpose of this book is to learn and better understand your camouflaging behaviours, and how these may be affecting your life, for good and bad. You might already know this, or you might have no idea if you have or haven't camouflaged before. Either is fine, and no matter your current level of awareness, I hope some of the exercises and strategies presented in the next few chapters might help you in some way, they certainly did me when I was first presented with them. To start with, this chapter helps you to look at specific camouflaging traits that you might be using, the contexts you might be using them in, and the possible reasons why you might be using them. By doing this you will gain more insight into your own strategies, which will not only help with your own understanding of your camouflaging and self, but also with future exercises in this book. It then goes on to explore how those strategies might be making you feel, and if there are any situations you find them particularly difficult to use in. Again, this is not about eliminating all your camouflaging strategies, as sometimes they might be actually making you feel more confident, it's about identifying which behaviours and which situations might be affecting your wellbeing.

You might find it stressful to start with thinking about all the ways you've camouflaged previously. However, it's important that we don't view our camouflaging as something we've done wrong, or something we've purposefully set out to do to 'trick' others. Camouflaging is a natural response to the social stressors and traumas many of us have experienced in our lives, and really we've only been tricking ourselves. It's important that as you start to explore and discover your own camouflaging traits you understand them as adaptive responses you have learned to keep you safe, both socially and emotionally. There is no turning back the clock and doing things differently; your brain took over and did what it needed to do so that you could survive and become the strong person you are today. Some of these strategies may have even enabled many positive things to happen in your life.

As I was an undiagnosed child my mum would often push me into 'play dates' with the children of her friends. I was incredibly socially anxious and would never have had the confidence or motivation to engage with them myself. Instead, I sat sullenly in the corner, completely mute until I was taken home where I could truly be my loud and relaxed self again. I guess these girls showed me how to play and socialise with other children in a 'non-autistic' way. I learned how they spoke, what they spoke about, what sorts of things they enjoyed, what was appropriate to say and what wasn't. I learned the hard way that people don't like it when you get extremely hyper and shout random words in their face, that people don't want to hear a monologue about the mundane conversation you had with the teacher over a pair of shoes. Equally, though, something I have struggled with even as an adult, is that people do want to hear your stories and experiences. Finding the balance of a two-way conversation remains a lifelong challenge for me. Too many times I've felt myself being too quiet in a conversation and having to quickly add a completely irrelevant or boring story, just to play my 'role' and to keep the conversation going.

As I got older I practised and rehearsed these conversations, I played out situation after situation so that I would never have to again experience the social awkwardness that came with silence and the darting of eyes as your conversation partner tries to find any excuse to leave. I even learned to make my eye contact look less irregular, counting it out so it went on for long enough, but making sure I looked away often enough that it was never so intense that I was mistaken for a psychopath. So immersed was I in this unconscious social dance that I rarely heard what the person was actually saying to me.

To add to the mountain of non-verbal communication distractors, I then realised people move their arms and hands when they spoke too. Every time I watched a person talking my focus was automatically drawn to studying their hands. Eventually I felt enough confidence to start adding this in to my own repertoire of communicative behaviours. Steadily these grew and built until they became more and more automatic, and until I could use them in many different types of situations other than the ones I had learned them in.

> *Bethany became much more aware that they were using camouflaging after receiving their diagnosis. In their teen years Bethany used it a lot as a coping mechanism without even realising, finding it helped ease a lot of social interactions. Bethany describes using forced vocal intonation to get rid of 'monotone speech' and using hand gestures and exacerbated facial features. Bethany views this as being in a drama and having to act in different situations. Because of this Bethany developed different personas, such as a 'work persona', 'Brownie Leader persona', and a 'university persona'.*

Even today, an adult in my 30s, I continue to monitor others and adapt my own communication. Recently I picked up that my speech perhaps doesn't have the same variety of inflection and pitch as others' does, or to put it more bluntly as my psychologist reported, I'm relatively "monotone with a flattened affect". Despite having worked on reducing my camouflaging for years now, I still automatically find myself listening to the speech patterns and sounds others made, and noticing my own voice adapt in response.

I have always studied people. While I had several 'special interests', these weren't anything you'd consider under the 'classic autistic behaviour' umbrella. I didn't particularly like trains or understanding physical systems or numbers. Instead I was obsessed with understanding humans as systems. How each part of their bodies moved in time with each other, how they dressed differently and adapted their mannerisms across different situations, but ultimately how they acted in a way that made other people like them. At 14 I was utterly obsessed with the popstar P!nk. While for many this obsession seemed normal – all teenagers fixate on people they like – as an autistic person this was a step up from your everyday run of the mill 'crush'. I was fixated. I obsessed over everything she did and said and I couldn't get enough. I tried to dress like her, I fantasised about growing my hair in blonde and pink dreadlocks, and I needed to collect everything about her. A similar fascination with Eminem earlier in my childhood hadn't turned out quite so well, so I imagine my parents were thankful for this slightly more appropriate fixation.

I also learned humour was the key to getting other people to like me, and I credit my development of sarcasm as a second language as the sole reason I am alive and kicking today, surrounded by people who now love and accept me for who I am, while equally being sick to death of my attempts to try and be funny in all situations. Perhaps I use humour to mitigate having to express emotions I'm not so keen on. Or perhaps I don't quite know what behaviour is socially acceptable in those situations so I fall back on often self-deprecating and distracting humour. Perhaps there is no perhaps about it; both of those things are definitely true.

Through the friendships born from these early social studies of mine I grew confidence to make more friendships, and go places and do things I'd have been too afraid to do alone. Even at university I hid away in my bedroom, sick to my stomach with nerves every day, but the group of friends I had made showed me how to adapt and, ultimately, how to survive being away from home with strangers. That meant I was able to finish my degree and had the confidence to apply to do my PhD. During my PhD studies I again hid myself away, too scared to meet new people and certainly too fearful to present my work to others. However, by observing others giving presentations of their work, monitoring how they sounded, what they looked like, and the kinds of things they'd say, I too grew the confidence to speak publicly. Doing so has led me to a wonderful group of fellow autistic allies and friends.

The point I want to portray is not that I would never have achieved what I did without camouflaging, it is that I couldn't help but camouflage as I grew up and adapted to the non-autistic environment around me. There have been pros to my camouflaging, but there have been many cons too. Autistic people *should* be able to achieve the things they want in their lives without having to adaptively morph into a person that does not come naturally to them. But unfortunately the fact of the matter is that for many of us this just isn't possible, so camouflaging helps us to survive when society is not ready to help us. As adults, however, we can choose to change this. First though, we need to explore your camouflaging behaviours and when they most often occur.

Christina didn't realise she was autistic until the age of 38. Up until that point she hadn't understood what masking was or that she was unconsciously doing it. Looking back on her childhood, she remembers feeling like other children "had access to some kind of mysterious manual of interactions that [she] hadn't been privy to". She realised she felt very drained after prolonged social interactions, not just because of the masking itself, but also because she was constantly trying to judge by others' reactions whether her 'performance' was acceptable. This caused her to look for work as a freelancer, rather than work full time in a studio setting, because it greatly reduces the length and amount of social interactions needed in a day. Christina also describes how, in informal social situations, she will tend to sit back and observe rather than forcing herself to take part. Conversely, she does enjoy public speaking – presentations are a different and more controlled experience.

Camouflaging Autistic Traits Questionnaire

The Camouflaging Autistic Traits Questionnaire, or CAT-Q for short, was developed by Hull and colleagues (2019) at University College London (UCL) and is reproduced below with permission. The questionnaire has 25 items on it, which tap into three elements of camouflaging. The first of these is compensation, which means using strategies that overcome difficulties in social situations, such as learning conversation responses ahead of social situations. Next is masking, which means using strategies to hide autistic traits, such as supressing stimming in public. Finally, the questionnaire also measures assimilation, which means using strategies to try and 'fit in' with others, such as feeling the need to act differently in order for others to like us. This is the first, and currently only, self-reporting questionnaire that measures camouflaging behaviours as a whole.

★ **Camouflaging Autistic Traits Questionnaire and scoring**

How to score your answers

Give the following score to each item that does *not* have an asterisk* beside it:

Strongly disagree:	1
Disagree:	2
Somewhat disagree:	3
Neither agree nor disagree:	4
Somewhat agree:	5
Agree:	6
Strongly agree:	7

Give the following score to each item that *does* have an asterisk* beside it:

Strongly disagree:	7
Disagree:	6
Somewhat disagree:	5
Neither agree nor disagree:	4
Somewhat agree:	3
Agree:	2
Strongly agree:	1

Take the CAT-Q!

Please read each statement below and choose the answer that best fits your experiences during social interactions.

	Strongly disagree	Disagree	Somewhat disagree	Neither agree nor disagree	Somewhat agree	Agree	Strongly agree
1. When I am interacting with someone, I deliberately copy their body language or facial expressions							
2. I monitor my body language or facial expressions so that I appear relaxed							
3. I rarely feel the need to put on an act in order to get through a social situation*							
4. I have developed a script to follow in social situations (for example, a list of questions or topics of conversation)							
5. I will repeat phrases that I have heard others say in the exact same way that I first heard them							
6. I adjust my body language or facial expressions so that I appear interested by the person I am interacting with							
7. In social situations, I feel like I'm 'performing' rather than being myself							
8. In my own social interactions, I use behaviours that I have learned from watching other people interacting							

cont.

	Strongly disagree	Disagree	Somewhat disagree	Neither agree nor disagree	Somewhat agree	Agree	Strongly agree
9. I always think about the impression I make on other people							
10. I need the support of other people in order to socialise							
11. I practise my facial expressions and body language to make sure they look natural							
12. I don't feel the need to make eye contact with other people if I don't want to*							
13. I have to force myself to interact with people when I am in social situations							
14. I have tried to improve my understanding of social skills by watching other people							
15. I monitor my body language or facial expressions so that I appear interested by the person I am interacting with							
16. When in social situations, I try to find ways to avoid interacting with others							
17. I have researched the rules of social interactions (for example, by studying psychology or reading books on human behaviour) to improve my own social skills							

18. I am always aware of the impression I make on other people					
19. I feel free to be myself when I am with other people*					
20. I learn how people use their bodies and faces to interact by watching television or films, or by reading fiction					
21. I adjust my body language or facial expressions so that I appear relaxed					
22. When talking to other people, I feel like the conversation flows naturally*					
23. I have spent time learning social skills from television shows and films, and try to use these in my interactions					
24. In social interactions, I do not pay attention to what my face or body are doing*					
25. In social situations, I feel like I am pretending to be 'normal'					

* Asterisked items are reverse scored compared to the other items. This is done in research to ensure participants don't go through ticking the same response to all items, and encourages them to read each question carefully before responding.

Item	Score		Item	Score		Item	Score
1			10			19	
2			11			20	
3			12			21	
4			13			22	
5			14			23	
6			15			24	
7			16			25	
8			17				
9			18			**TOTAL**	

Scores range from 25 to 175, but there is no set score for what constitutes 'high camouflaging' and what constitutes 'low camouflaging', although scores over 100 tend to indicate stronger camouflaging. In their paper studying the scale, Hull and colleagues (2020) found that there were not only some significant differences between autistic people and non-autistic people, but also between males and females. Add up the total points you scored and have a look at this table of average scores and see where yours fits.

Typical scores on the CAT-Q (Hull *et al.* 2019)

Autistic		Non-autistic	
Female	Male	Female	Male
124	110	91	97

You might want to keep taking this test as you work through the following chapters. There may be some camouflaging behaviours in the scale that you weren't even aware you did, alternatively you might find that the more aware you become and the more you work to reduce some of the more problematic ones, the lower your score gets.

When and why do you camouflage?

While the CAT-Q can tell us a great deal about the different ways in which we might be camouflaging, it can't tell us why, when, or how often we are camouflaging. This is important for us to be aware of, for reasons that will become clearer in the next chapter.

> *Jenny began camouflaging while at school to make sure other children wouldn't make fun of her. While she didn't find this helped avoid ridicule, as an adult she continues to use it to help herself get through situations easily and to help keep going. She described having to put on a 'mask' to temporarily bury her own struggles to be there for her children at times too. Jenny has found camouflaging makes her feel "confident and competent" but exhausted too if she does it for too long or too often.*

Cage and Troxell-Whitman (2019) reviewed the current literature on the topic of camouflaging and devised a list of reasons why people camouflage, as well as the contexts in which people camouflage. Reasons for camouflaging were found to fall into two broader categories: conventional reasons, whereby individuals used camouflaging to get by at work or at school, and relational reasons, whereby individuals used camouflaging to get by in social situations with others. Contexts for camouflaging were also found to fall into two broader categories: in formal situations, such as when around professionals, and in interpersonal situations, such as when around friends and family.

One of the difficulties of trying to measure camouflaging is that we can only measure what we're consciously aware of, and many of our camouflaging behaviours happen at an unconscious level. Most people automatically attempt to synchronise their behaviours to those around them, and more often than not they are unaware that this is happening (Wiltermuth & Heath 2009). You can see this at work when you watch two people talking and at similar times they cross their arms or legs, or start to smile when they see the other person laughing or smiling. It is likely that if you asked these people, "Were you intentionally imitating?" they would be entirely unaware of those behaviours. The same goes for autistic camouflaging: much of what you do happens at such an unconscious level it would take some time for you to recognise you've been doing it. It's important to point out here, though, that there's nothing wrong with any of these behaviours; we'd never suggest that non-autistic people stop automatically mirroring the behaviour of others. If anything, it acts as a social 'glue' during these interactions. What's problematic is camouflaging behaviours that take your time and energy, and which you feel you have to do to ensure others like you and don't perceive your differences. It's working out which behaviours cause you more cons than pros. Over time thinking about your behaviours you'll gain a better insight into yourself, and the benefit of this is that you can start to become your own advocate; you can control how you want to be and when.

Exercises

The studies on camouflaging presented in this chapter are just interpretations of what camouflaging looks like for lots of autistic people, based on psychological research. However, your experience of camouflaging may be very different. Hopefully filling in the CAT-Q has got you thinking about your own strategies and when and why you use them. Using the space below jot down any other thoughts you have about what camouflaging strategies you've used in the past or are using now. Try and recollect what situations they occurred in and how often you use them too.

YOUR EXAMPLES

Example: I remember when I was younger I used to wear my brother's clothes so that I looked just like him. I mainly did this at home because I wanted to be like him, but when I went to school I felt too embarrassed to dress like this and wore more 'girly' clothing to fit in with my friends.

. . . .

. . . .

. . . .

. . . .

. . . .

. . . .

. . . .

. . . .

It is all well and good being aware and understanding how and when you're camouflaging, but how does it actually make you feel? More importantly, what effect is it having on your life? As I mentioned previously, sometimes using these strategies might make you feel super confident and like you can take on the world; at other times, however, they might leave you feeling pretty drained and feeling bad about yourself. For me, when I leave a talk I've given to lots of people I often feel on top of the world, I feel energised by the connection I made with the audience and pleased with how I presented myself. But there are many more times when, for example, I come away from seeing friends and find myself plagued with a nagging feeling of something not being right. I feel mute as I rack my brain ruminating over all the things I did and said wrong, about how they must have seen me, and ultimately about the lasting impression I left.

Cognitive behavioural therapy (CBT) is a fairly popular branch of psychotherapy that targets and challenges a person's unhelpful thoughts and behaviours (Beck 2011). There are a few simple tools we can take away from this method that might help us to better understand how our own camouflaging behaviour is affecting us. The first of these explores a specific situation, the thoughts and feelings you had in that situation, any bodily sensations you felt, your mood and emotions at the time, and behaviours you did or didn't do as a result. If you're anything like me then you may find labelling your exact emotions pretty tricky! Many of us also experience *alexithymia*, which results in difficulties identifying and describing emotions, making any attempts at CBT feel like you're hitting a brick wall repeatedly. However, by trying these exercises again and again, and just filling in what you can every time, the 'work' will be happening. I have filled in hundreds of these sheets, and I can now guess my emotions based on what the bodily sensations I report are and what kind of thoughts I am having. I know that if I have a funny feeling in my throat, I'm probably feeling sad. Similarly, I know that if I start thinking "What did they think of me?" I'm probably feeling quite anxious. It's perfectly OK to start labelling your feelings in this way, and gradually over time you may even start finding you become a natural at interpreting them without needing to do this. Let's walk through this step by step with some examples.

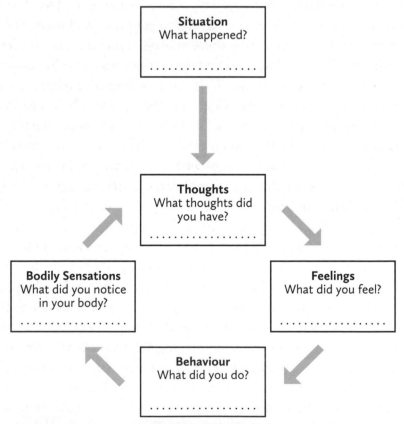

Figure 3.1 Situation, thoughts, feelings, and behaviour diagram

1. *Identify a situation* in which you've recently camouflaged. This could be any occasion, but be specific.
   - For example, yesterday I met with two close friends in their garden for lunch.
2. *Think about the thoughts you had at the time.* List as many as you can remember, good and bad.
   - Using the example I gave above, some of the thoughts I had included "I feel like I'm looking weird", "Why can't I keep eye contact?", "They're going to notice", "They'll think I'm being different", "They'll think I'm bored", "I'm too tired", "I wish I could leave", "I'm no good at this".
3. *What body sensations did you notice?* This box can be a little more difficult to fill in. Sometimes when we are in these situations we cope by switching off all our feelings, both physical and mental, to give our full concentration to coping with the situation.
   - I noticed in this situation, in my friend's garden, that I suddenly became very tired. I also noticed my throat had begun feeling a bit tight, I'd lost my appetite, and I was having difficulty eating my lunch.
4. *What feelings did you notice?* Again, this can be a tricky one. Often we camouflage so automatically we don't have time to notice any feelings. You might be able to figure this out based on what your thoughts were at the time or your bodily sensations.
   - I think I must have been anxious in this social situation. When I get very anxious I tend to start shutting down and getting tired, and I also get a lump in my throat which may have been making it hard for me to eat. I think I felt quite sad too, because I felt like I'd failed at what should have been a normal social event.
5. *Remember how you responded in this situation.* This is the most important part of the cycle and one we'll return to later. Here we can identify what your coping mechanisms are, whether they're useful, or whether they may be perpetuating this cycle.
   - I stayed in this situation as I didn't want anyone to notice

my anxiety. I tried to force myself to make eye contact, I tried to chat more enthusiastically, asking more questions. I tried to stim and fiddle less too. I went on to spend time with another friend afterwards because I didn't want to cancel and make them change their plans. The next day I hid in bed and was exhausted.

The more times you fill in this diagram, the more awareness you'll gain. Perhaps spend a solid week filling one of these in every time you encounter a social situation, and see which situations seem to cause you the most negative feelings. You might notice patterns too. Perhaps you experience more negative emotions when you've had several social events in a row, whereas when you socialise after spending several days resting, you find you don't experience such negative feelings. It may be that one day I feel relatively fine after attending a large gathering with lots of people I don't know, such as a birthday party. Yet meeting a close friend for coffee might make me withdraw into myself and want to escape the situation faster than leaving a group meeting when someone's just started a round of icebreakers. Similarly, one day I can manage a large supermarket shop, and another I can barely leave the house to walk to the post box. It often feels like there is no pattern to our anxiety and we cannot predict how events will make us feel from one day to the next. But really there are always signs and reasons; we have most probably just suppressed them and not appreciated our triggers at the time. From looking at my examples in this cycle I can see that my decision to camouflage my anxiety, and even to go on to socialise more after this first event, would have contributed to my overwhelm the next day. My priority was to please others here. I was worried what they would think of me, and ultimately that I would disappoint them. Perhaps even that I would lose my friends, rather than worrying about my own wellbeing. A commonly used metaphor is that of a bucket that continually gets filled until eventually it is overflowing. If we apply this to our use of camouflaging in social situations you can see how each occasion might add to that bucket. The first social event I went to filled the bucket almost to the brim, the second event may have only induced a little anxiety and pressure to camouflage but this was enough to make me spill over the following day. 'Shut down' is a common experience for many autistic people, which can result from severe exhaustion. Reasons include sensory overload, social situations, camouflaging, suppressing stims, and feeling like you're not meeting others' expectations. You may find you go quite quiet, struggling to communicate with even those close to you as a result.

Ideally, we want to find a balance in our lives where we can still attend these social situations and feel we are being successful in them, but where they don't cause ourselves to completely burn out. In the following chapters we'll explore strategies that you might find useful to help you reduce some of these negative fallouts from camouflaging. My advice at this point would be not to rush through the chapters, or if you do want to do this then plan to come back and revisit some of these exercises at the end. It'll be important to have as much evidence and awareness of your camouflaging as possible before you tackle some of the later strategies this book will introduce.

KEY MESSAGES

- Being more aware of which camouflaging strategies you use could help you gain more insight into your behaviours and relationships.
- High camouflagers tend to camouflage lots in all contexts, while some people may switch to camouflage highly in one situation but less so in another.
- Because our experiences are all so different, with different autistic traits and environments, your camouflaging strategies may be unique to you.
- CBT methods, like the behaviour and thought cycle introduced here, will help you to better understand the effects camouflaging is having on you, and what coping mechanisms you currently use.

CHAPTER 4

How to Be Self-Compassionate

CHAPTER'S PURPOSE
To learn methods of managing overwhelming
feelings and to practise self-compassion
to reduce anxiety and depression.

KEY TERMS
- *Thinking errors:* Automatic thoughts that aren't necessarily based in reality
- *DBT:* Dialectic behaviour therapy, which is used for managing intense feelings
- *Distress tolerance:* Our ability to manage overwhelming feelings and distress

In the next chapter we'll look at ways you can start reducing your camouflaging. But, for now, let's sit with this newfound knowledge and awareness of how you've been camouflaging and the feelings you might have from the last chapter. You might have always known this stuff, but it's likely that even reading and reminding yourself of sources of stress in your life will have triggered some uncomfortable memories and feelings. Fortunately, this makes for an excellent time in your journey to start thinking about compassion for yourself, and how this might look in practice. There are a number of techniques in this chapter that will prepare you better for the next stage of your journey, one where you might want to consider practising taking off the mask and reducing your camouflaging.

> *Kayleigh, who was finally diagnosed at 18, felt that she masked a lot growing up because she "always felt different and was bullied if [she] showed it both at home and in school". Masking allowed her to "fit in" in these difficult environments. Since her diagnosis she has been able to stop masking as much at home with her partner, describing it as a "safe space" where she isn't judged. The key technique she has used that has enabled her to do this is by being more compassionate to herself. She described how she has "flashbacks to past events and by addressing them and giving [her] younger self love and compassion for things that happened", she felt "less guilty for being 'herself' and having some difficulties". When she does have to mask she tries to counteract the negative effects of this by taking time out for "self-care and rest" afterwards.*

I have to confess, this was the hardest chapter of this book to write. Even reading the words 'self-compassion' and 'mindfulness' made me want to immediately close whatever book or article I was reading. It's easy to think of ways to be compassionate to other people, but it's much more difficult to consider how we can be compassionate to ourselves. It can also be the most difficult skill to acquire when your mind is set on berating yourself for every social mistake you make and is fixated on trying to make others happy.

The word 'compassion' stems from two Latin words which mean 'to suffer' and 'with', therefore compassion really just means to 'suffer with'. It goes beyond sympathy of what that suffering is, and evokes an empathic response of also feeling that suffering too. The first and most important act of our self-compassion then is to just acknowledge and feel our suffering. What does this look like in reality? It can be as simple as having an understanding of ourselves and what we've been through, of not judging ourselves to high and unachievable standards, and being as forgiving of ourselves as we are to others. If your friend was to make a social faux pas the chances are you probably wouldn't even notice, or if you did you'd probably comfort them and tell them it really doesn't matter. Why, then, when we make a similar social faux pas do we feel like the world has ended? The real battle many of us have with self-compassion is that many of us are also highly depressed and anxious as a result of our constant need to camouflage. We face self-critical thoughts and ruminations daily that inhibit our ability to have any self-compassion at all. Which is why we need to retrain our brains to be self-compassionate; we need to actively force ourselves to practise strategies that will eventually make us more rational and compassionate beings.

Why is this important when it comes to camouflaging? As discussed in Chapter 2, camouflaging has a whole host of negative mental health consequences, and a lifetime of camouflaging will have led to us collecting buckets full of self-criticism. Dr Katherina Hamm regularly works with clients who have found themselves camouflaging to survive, at the expense of their mental health and wellbeing. In discussions with me she explains how increased anxiety can often make us camouflage even more, so we end up in a vicious cycle where we camouflage to cope with those social anxieties only to find ourselves more depressed and anxious as a result. She describes this as being like a soldier adding more and more camouflaging gear to their uniform until they're weighed down by the sheer heaviness and become virtually unrecognizable. However, by reducing our shame and by being more compassionate our anxiety will reduce and with it our need to camouflage as much. As we take off the layers of our camouflage we are lessening the load and the resources we need to maintain it.

In his book *The Compassionate Mind* (2009) Professor Paul Gilbert provides an excellent account of how our different brain systems often operate in conflict with one another, detailing how we can overcome many of the problems this creates by practising more compassion for ourselves. Our basic emotion systems, also known as our 'old brain', has been operating in all species for millennia. Its main drive has been to protect us from danger. Any perceived threat overrides all our other systems, including our soothing and contentment system, and prepares us for 'flight or fight' (our reaction to danger). The problem with this 'old brain', particularly in modern times, is that its reactions are often no longer relevant or helpful. We may experience automatic negative emotions in response to our perceived social failure, for example it can make us feel like an outsider and disconnect us from others. Unlike other species, however, humans have evolved a 'new brain'. This is one that gives us the propensity to develop language and think in symbols. This is the system I described in Chapter 1, which enables us to operate in social environments, to imagine and plan ahead both individually and as a group. We possess an incredible ability to learn new things and for our brains to continually change throughout our lives as a result of this 'new brain'. There is a danger, however, when the new brain collides with the old brain when we are not aware. Many of our 'new brain' fantasies activate our 'old brain' threat systems and drive us to anxiety and depression. Take for instance a fear of embarrassing yourself in public, perhaps by saying the wrong thing or missing an important social cue: when you're in social situations that imagined scenario will trigger the 'old brain' and create fear. Or perhaps you're often comparing yourself to others, watching how they behave and comparing it to your own social performance. This triggers more negative emotions from our 'old brains', such as inferiority and worthlessness. The true art of compassion is to stand back from this 'old brain' and to non-judgementally assess its reaction. Too often we trust and believe our feelings and emotions, we justify them to make sense of them, and we very rarely question their existence. In fact, 'trust your gut' is often the advice we give each other when we cannot make a decision. What we should be telling each other instead is to ignore our gut and instead think more compassionately. Gilbert (2009) describes some of the attributes and skills needed for compassion, including being more mindful and remembering experiences of compassion, being more in tune with our feelings, tolerating rather than avoiding feelings, and being more accepting and less condemning of our self and others.

Fionnuala, a clinical psychologist, has experience of working with autistic adults to help them reduce their need to camouflage. She suggests "working through feelings of stigma and shame".

For example, many autistic people have received negative reactions from others while growing up regarding their behaviour, however, by learning to think and feel differently about experiences and developing self-compassion, you can stop blaming yourself for others' reactions to you. She says, "Becoming more accepting, compassionate, and proud of yourself can be helpful, and can mean that confronting other people's (sometimes) negative reactions may not feel as painful." Additionally, Fionnuala mentioned the importance of trying to be "upfront about your differences". By letting people know about your needs in advance it can relieve some of the pressure you may feel to 'perform' and hide those differences. Fionnuala believes that society is becoming increasingly accepting of neurodiversity, however, she stresses the importance of not blaming or attacking yourself should you encounter someone who is not tolerant of your differences. Last, she suggests that: "Having allies and people you can confide in when you feel hurt or tired out by other people can be helpful to feel connected and supported."

One of the difficulties I have always faced when it comes to self-compassion is that it feels slightly abstract; I couldn't see how it would change me or benefit my life. I embarked on a scientific journey to really get to grips with what compassion was, and the evidence was staggering. Neuroscientist Professor Olga Klimecki and colleagues (2013) identified that compassion-based training was able to reverse the negative effects experienced by participants watching videos depicting human suffering. Not only this, but increased activations were observed in brain regions associated with emotion, decision making, and reward-related behaviour. The authors concluded that compassion-based training can actually enable individuals to acquire a new coping strategy to overcome empathic distress and also increase resilience. Dr Fiona Ashworth has practised these methods in clinical settings to determine if they can actually help patients improve their mood. Ashworth and colleagues (2014) identified that patients with brain injuries, who subsequently experienced psychological distress, demonstrated improvements in anxiety, depression and self-criticism, and an improved ability to reassure themselves after having compassion-focused therapy. So it would seem that self-compassion isn't just some airy fairy modern notion to temporarily make ourselves feel better, but in fact a concrete tool for altering our state of mind at a biological level. The more we practise using these parts of our brain, the more resilient and compassionate we become.

In his book, Gilbert (2009) draws on a cycle of grief to conceptualise how experiences of criticism may lead us to feeling isolated and alone. This motivates us to criticise ourselves and change our behaviours to ensure others like us, resulting in feelings of depression as we internalise the feelings of anger we have towards others. Psychotherapist Sigmund Freud often spoke of depression as anger turned inwards (Freud 1962). After all, if we are desperate to be liked by others around us, we don't want them to know we are angry with them. Inspired by this cycle, I have drawn Figure 4.1 showing we could apply this to camouflaging.

According to Gilbert (2009), a crucial step in breaking this cycle is to understand that the criticism we received from others in the past is not fact, and possibly no longer relevant in our lives at all. This can be extremely difficult to do; we have spent our lives putting others first and trying to appease and please them. We possibly no longer even feel that we deserve compassion. When therapists suggested I be kinder to myself I often replied "But why?" I didn't feel I'd done anything to deserve that kindness. I felt like I was pandering to myself, spoiling myself with undeserving and self-indulgent praise. But it is not this at all, the core elements of compassion are sensitivity and sympathy towards our distress. It's a necessity for our health, not a luxury we can afford to ignore. More on how to tackle this in a bit, but for now we just need to better understand exactly how we've been judging ourselves and what sort of thinking traps we may have fallen into over time as a consequence.

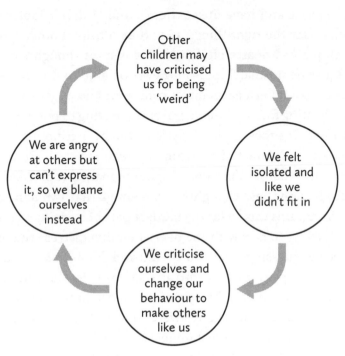

Figure 4.1 Cycle of grief

The power of thoughts

We can't change what others have thought about us in the past, we can only change what we think about ourselves now. In order to tackle our inner self-critic we need to pay attention to what it's saying first. Once we know what it's saying, we need to change the language it uses and turn it into a more compassionate voice. Remember, the more you practise self-compassion, the more activated your brain will become in areas that will better support your wellbeing, which will hopefully become automatic after a while.

In the last chapter we mapped out some specific situations in which you'd felt the need to camouflage, and how these had made you feel and act. If you focus now on the 'thoughts' box of Figure 3.1, you might start to see some common automatic thoughts you've been having. For example, looking back on all my past worksheets I've noticed that my most common thoughts tend to be "Everyone's leaving me out because they don't like me", "I've said something inappropriate and have upset them", and "I didn't look excited enough or say the right things, now they'll think I don't care". All these thoughts are often followed by constant thoughts of "Why can't I just be normal?" and "I'll never be able to do this." Every now and then it permeates into a contempt and anger that others aren't adjusting for my 'differences' or not having to put in the same effort I am. But these are swiftly followed by a crippling sense of depression and detachment from any feelings at all. Sometimes I'm not sure whether I'm camouflaging to make people like me, or to avoid having these thoughts and feelings that I've done something wrong. This was by far the hardest part of learning to unmask myself, having to deal with the overwhelming distress that comes with second guessing what you've said and done. This is also why I would never suggest rushing into all these exercises and attempting to unmask immediately. The process is more important than the end result, and becoming more aware, and gradually lowering those barriers, will be far more sustainable and healthy in the long run.

Using the table on the following page start to think of some of your own automatic thoughts. It's easiest to think of a situation first, like the ones we identified in the last exercise in Chapter 3, and then come up with a list of thoughts that went with them. Ignore the greyed out 'New thought' column, we'll come back to this in a bit.

★ **Situations and automatic thoughts**

Situation/trigger	Automatic thoughts	New thought
Example: I forgot to ask my friend how she was when I bumped into her yesterday	"She's going to think I'm really selfish" "She'll think I don't care" "She seems off, it's because I didn't ask her" "I should know how to have a conversation" "I need to speak to her again so I can rectify this" "She won't want to be my friend" "I feel like an idiot"	

Before we start to look at how to change these thoughts, it's worth spending some time identifying any common thinking errors you might be falling into. In CBT, thinking errors are defined as a faulty pattern of thinking that has negative consequences (Ellis 1957). Usually these thoughts aren't grounded in reality and are instead distortions of the truth. Without breaking this cycle of thinking errors it will be quite difficult for us to replace our self-critical thoughts with more compassionate ones.

Ignoring the good: The first of these thinking errors involves only focusing on the negative. In the example I have given above I have ocused on one error I have made: not asking my friend how she was. There is no mention of the perfectly pleasant conversation we had where I did ask her a few questions about herself. I have ignored the good parts of this conversation and only focused on the negative. This is also known as a cognitive bias, and is quite a common error made by people who are depressed and anxious.

Blowing things up out of proportion: In the example given above you can see that one of my thoughts was that she wouldn't want to be my friend. However, the likelihood of this happening just because I didn't ask her how she was once is incredibly small. I've blown the situation up out of proportion, and what was a relatively small mistake has become huge with serious consequences.

Fortune telling: Another thinking error that goes with this thought is believing you know what will happen in the future. Here I am predicting that my friend won't like me any more, most probably based on some past experience I had when I was very young. It is not based in reality, I am using my automatic negative thoughts to predict the worst.

Mind reading: This means believing we know what someone else must be thinking even though we could not possibly ever do this. In this example I assume my friend will think I'm selfish and that she'll also think I don't care, when actually I have no evidence as to whether this is true or not. Again, it's very much based around my automatic negative thoughts.

Negative labelling: I have also gone on to say that I am an 'idiot' here for doing this, labelling the situation in a negative way. This means having a negative belief about yourself and therefore assuming it applies to everything you do. I have a deep fear of looking silly or people thinking this of me, and so it figures that anytime I feel I've messed up it triggers this thought.

Setting the bar too high: Another common thought error is thinking we always have to be perfect or otherwise we are worthless. In the example given I clearly believe that I need to be absolutely perfect or I will be no good at all as a friend. By making one mistake I have failed in this mission, however, this is a standard I would certainly not apply to my friends and their mistakes.

Self-blame: You can see here in my thought patterns that I am blaming myself for my friend seeming 'off'. I am making an assumption that this must be because of my social error and not because of any other factor in her life. I am ignoring all the other things that might be going on in her life at that moment and focusing only on myself as a factor.

Feelings as facts: I go on to think that I've messed up, that it's my fault and therefore that must be true. We often don't question our thoughts and feelings, assuming they must be real if we have experienced them. However, as you can see from all these examples of thinking errors, we often cannot trust what we think and feel; it is far from fact.

Should statements: Last, you will see in my example that I feel I *should* have known how to have this conversation perfectly. Again, this is an unrealistic expectation to have; in hindsight we might know what we should have done, but it isn't realistic to think we will always get everything perfectly right. We are setting ourselves up for failure.

Being compassionate means reflecting on these thinking errors in a gentle and sympathetic manner. It doesn't mean adding another thing to your list that you feel you're failing at – "Oh no, I can't even think correctly!" Remember, we have evolved to use these patterns in our thinking; they were designed to protect us. By noticing these thoughts and validating them you can begin to disrupt them. You can try writing down the situation, how you felt and what you thought, and then non-judgementally assess it. It's a good idea here to think of your strengths too and be supportive and empathic. For example, I've written the following about the situation I described above:

> When I bumped into my friend yesterday I forgot to ask her how she was, despite her asking me. I'm worrying that she's now think-ing I'm really selfish and impolite. Yesterday she didn't answer my text and I kept thinking she's being off with me because of our conversation. I feel really anxious she's not going to want me as a friend now, and I feel really annoyed with myself for not being able to interact with her how others would. I guess I feel like this because people told me in the past I was being impolite when I didn't mean to be, and now I really worry what others think of me. However, it was a really quick chat we had and I was overwhelmed as I hadn't been prepared to see her, so it's understandable that I didn't ask her lots of questions. My friends usually say I'm very thoughtful, and I make sure I always check in on them and ask how they are. I also remembered to ask her about her new job when we bumped into each other. I wonder if she is now worried she didn't ask me how my mum was because I told her last week she'd been unwell? If she was I'd tell her not to worry at all, it didn't bother me and it was such a quick conversation as she was rushing on her way to work. I guess this might be why she's not replying too; if she's very stressed from working at her new job she probably hasn't even thought about what we spoke about when we bumped into each other.

The best way to break these thinking errors is to start noticing them and replacing them. Using the table you completed of your automatic thoughts, go through and try and identify which thinking errors you think apply to each of your thoughts. Once you've identified those we can start to change and rewrite these thoughts. Using the same table we used above, we can now fill in the greyed out 'New thought' column. The table is repeated on the following page, and there I've included some more examples to give you an idea of what kinds of things you could write here. To begin with this task might feel a little forced and unnatural; sometimes it takes consciously doing something over and over before it becomes an automatic habit we do naturally. I suggest keeping a diary where you write down and challenge your thoughts daily. Remember, your new thoughts should avoid self-blame and assumptions, and focus instead on more compassionate ways of viewing the situation. Sometimes it's easier to imagine what you would tell a friend if they'd told you they were having these thoughts. We would often automatically respond with empathy and try and reassure them that what they had done wasn't as awful as they thought or, even if they had made a mistake, we would be supportive in helping them to resolve this.

Hopefully this exercise has got you thinking about some of the ways you may have been thinking overly critically of yourself. While there are lots of practical activities that can help us grow our self-compassion, they're pretty pointless if we still keep thinking we are terrible people who ruin everything with everyone! There are lots of other activities you can do to help tackle self-critical and negative thoughts – if this is an area you'd like to explore more then I'd thoroughly recommend reading *Mind Over Mood* by Dr Greenberger and Dr Padesky (2016). The next section will take a look at how we can learn to manage difficult emotions that often come with those thoughts.

★ Creating new compassionate thoughts to our automatic thoughts

Situation/trigger	Automatic thoughts	New 'compassionate' thought
Example: I forgot to ask my friend how she was when I bumped into her yesterday	"She's going to think I'm really selfish" "She'll think I don't care" "She seems off, it's because I didn't ask her" "I should know how to have a conversation" "I need to speak to her again so I can rectify this" "She won't want to be my friend" "I feel like an idiot"	"I made one little mistake and even if she did notice I'm sure she has made similar mistakes before too and would understand" "The rest of the conversations went very well and I did ask her how her job was going" "It was only a short conversation as we were passing each other, so it doesn't matter that I didn't ask her everything" "She's been my friend for several years now and never not wanted to be friends with me before over something I think I've done or said wrong" "She was probably feeling quite stressed and tired and that's why she seemed 'off'" "I did my best in this situation and it doesn't matter that I made one little mistake"

Distress tolerance

As I mentioned previously, a big problem with learning to be more compassionate is having to sit with, and deal with, emotions that feel overwhelming. You might find you try and avoid these negative feelings as much as possible. For example, feeling like you've upset someone or that you've been rejected by others hurts pretty badly. It can feel easier to avoid these feelings by behaving in ways that never disappoint people, to always say 'yes' to people, and hide your true feelings. This is the opposite of being compassionate to ourselves. A more compassionate self would instead sit with those negative feelings and watch as they pass by. It is a technique that has been the cornerstone of dialectic behavioural therapy (DBT), which is a type of CBT used for people who experience very intense emotions (Linehan *et al.* 1991). There are a few simple techniques described below that may help you regulate your distress better, which then in turn can help you be more compassionate and reduce your need to camouflage as much. However, if you find distress intolerance to be a bigger problem for you, you may want to consider approaching a DBT therapist for further help (www.findatherapist.co.uk).

First, start taking note of the negative feelings you find overwhelming and how you react to them. Using the table on the following page, you can identify each time you feel a negative emotion, how intolerable you find it, and how you react. I've filled in an example of a situation I have struggled with. In this scenario I became very anxious about having to give a talk at work in front of my colleagues. The days leading up to it felt utterly intolerable. I reacted by trying to shut down my feelings and avoid the situation, and eventually ended up feeling so unwell I had to call in sick. Avoiding the talk led to immediate relief, as if the pressure had just been instantly released. However, in the long term it affected my self-esteem and confidence at work. I felt guilty I'd let my colleagues down, I worried even more about the next time I'd need to give a talk, and generally I just felt like I'd failed. While sometimes it's perfectly OK to look after ourselves and not put ourselves into situations that we know we can't cope with, this wasn't one of those situations. I avoided this situation purely to relieve myself of the intolerable anxiety I was experiencing.

★ **Negative emotions and reactions**

What is the negative emotion?	How intolerable is it? (0–5)	What did you do?
Anxiety	4	Tried to stop the feelings and avoided discussing it with anyone. Ended up becoming too physically unwell and having to call in sick on the day of the talk.

Now you've identified some of the emotions you've found intolerable, and some of the ways you have tried to cope with these, it's important to better understand the beliefs that drive these sorts of reactions. Typical beliefs include "I'm going to lose control", "I can't cope with this", and "It's wrong to feel this way." In the scenario I gave above I held many of these beliefs, including the belief that I needed to immediately stop the anxiety or the feeling would go on forever. It's not uncommon for people to even hurt themselves to relieve some of these feelings. The issue with holding these beliefs, and the reactions we have to them, is that they can be more harmful than the negative emotion itself. It goes without saying that physically harming ourselves is damaging, but so too is avoiding or trying to numb feelings, as we end up missing out on a lot of positive and enjoyable emotions too. It is also likely that you will find yourself dwelling on your reaction, feeling as though you can't cope, and fearing similar situations in the future. What we never give ourselves a chance to do is sit with our distress and challenge these beliefs. There is only one route out of distress intolerance, and unfortunately it's not a comfortable one!

Radical acceptance is the practice of accepting our emotional distress (Hayes, Strosahl, & Wilson 2012). This doesn't mean that we like it, it just means we accept it. It involves non-judgementally observing a bad feeling and letting it pass through. There are some simple mindfulness exercises you can do to help with this if you're struggling; they are described in the next section. Another technique you can use involves coaching yourself when you're feeling distressed. You can follow a simple script like the one below instead of trying to avoid or numb the feelings you experience.

What are you feeling?
My stomach has butterflies and I feel really weird, I think this must be anxiety.

Accept the feeling
This is OK and I can have this feeling, I don't need to try and get rid of it, it will pass on its own when it's ready. I'm going to just watch this

feeling and see where it goes, I am not my emotions and my emotions will not hurt me. This is just like a train passing through.

Focus on the present

I will focus on what I was doing, paying attention to my breath as I do it, the sounds I can hear, and the smells I can see.

What if it comes back?

I'm feeling another wave of anxiety rush through me, which is fine, it will go and come and I will just watch it again.

Try and fill in your own script next time you're feeling overwhelmed by your stress.

What are you feeling?

. . . .

. . . .

. . . .

. . . .

. . . .

Accept the feeling

. . . .

. . . .

. . . .

. . . .

. . . .

Focus on the present

. . . .

. . . .

. . . .

. . . .

. . . .

What if it comes back?

. . . .

. . . .

. . . .

. . . .

. . . .

Of course, this isn't an exact science and it may take you many attempts before you begin to feel it's making a difference. Try to avoid feeling like a failure when these techniques don't help you straight away; we are all different and therefore may require different strategies. When I was first introduced to distress intolerance the biggest problem I faced was being able to label and read my emotions in the first place. You may want to take some time focusing on the situation, thoughts, feelings, and behaviour diagram (Figure 3.1) in the last chapter. Sometimes it's easier to figure out our feelings by learning which bodily sensations and thoughts go with each emotion.

Listening to our distress and accepting it is the first step, but ultimately we want to improve it. The key to achieving this is to practise doing the opposite of whatever we were doing previously to avoid or get rid of the distress. Let's try and apply this to camouflaging behaviours to see how this could work. Sometimes I avoid going to new environments with people because I'm scared I'll be so anxious that I'll lose my mask in front of them. I get distressed just at the thought and can't make any plans because I know I won't be able to cope with the anxiety leading up to the event. This is avoidance, and while it may help me temporarily relieve the anxiety I have, it makes me feel pretty rubbish in the long run that I can't have exciting new experiences and that I keep letting people down. It also means I grow more and more scared of similar events and the anxiety they'll cause in the future. If I were to do the opposite of avoidance I would simply face this situation head on and go to these new environments, watching and observing my distress as I go until it passes. However, this is where these therapeutic techniques need to be adapted for autistic people. While a non-autistic person might face this situation and realise their anxiety at the feared event was not as bad as they predicted, this is often not as simple for autistic people. There is a neurobiological reason as to why we are sensitive to certain environments, be that sensory issues, social communication struggles, or difficulties coping with change. While the mantra 'feel the fear and do it anyway' has helped many non-autistic people overcome their fears, the less catchy autistic version should read more like 'feel the fear and then gradually make adaptations that help you to do it anyway, but only eventually when you're ready'. So my advice is not to jump in and immediately do everything you've avoided, but instead to work out a plan that feels acceptable to you, and which allows you to eventually be able to participate in the activity you've been avoiding. This could start by taking small steps, like going to a new location with a person you know well and trust, and then building this up. You might want to consult with a therapist to help you do this.

However you decide to tackle your avoidance or other harmful coping mechanisms, it's important that you also build in time for soothing activities after, doing something that makes you feel the opposite of distressed, something you know will calm you. This might be stimming with your favourite fidget toy, having a bath, doing some drawing, or watching your favourite TV show. Remember, with all these exercises you need to ensure you are being compassionate towards yourself and that you're not punishing yourself, no matter how unsuccessful you perceive yourself to have been on any particular exercise. Keep a record of how well these distress improvement activities go, like the one here.

★ **Monitoring distress improvement activities**

Distress improvement activity	What happened?	What did you learn?
For example: Stroked my cat	I got distracted, the anxiety still came and went, and when I stopped it came back, but for a few moments it eased	For a little while I forgot what I was distressed about, showing me it won't last forever

As with all these exercises, they only work if you continually practise them. Eventually your mind will automatically know how to tolerate your distress, and you'll know what you need to do in these situations to help it. If you've found these helpful you can try more distress tolerance exercises from the Centre for Clinical Interventions (www.cci.health.wa.gov.au).

Mindfulness and imagery

Mindfulness is perhaps one of the easiest and cheapest forms of therapy, and is a fantastic complement to the exercises described in this chapter. However, for some it can also be the hardest to master. My first introduction to mindfulness was not a success, and neither was my second, third, fourth, or fifth attempt. In fact, I gave up on it completely and decided that it didn't work for people like me. I struggled with the abstractness of it, having to imagine colours and various images, not to mention the constant negative voice in my head that would narrate the entire exercise and distract me with any thought it could muster from the pits of my memory bank – "Remember that time you tripped at school? This would be a great time to think about that again." After reading more on the science behind mindfulness I decided to give it another try, but this time in a more structured setting where someone could guide me through the exercises. I embarked on a weekend mindfulness retreat. Since then I have been a keen advocate of the practice, and have seen the benefits it has had on both my body and my mind. When I feel anxiety and exhaustion rising I'm often able to stop it in its tracks.

The practice itself has been around for thousands of years. Put simply, it is a meditative state of being aware of your present surroundings, feelings, and bodily sensations. In the 1970s mindfulness entered the Western world, and since then has been empirically studied and used for the treatment of many physiological and psychological problems, most notably anxiety and depression (Shonin *et al.* 2015). While mindfulness is a mental practice, research has shown that it works by changing our neurobiology, making us more attentive to the present moment, and therefore less ruminative of previous events that have caused distress (Tang, Hölzel, & Posner 2015). Evidence has found it can affect brain plasticity, which is the brain's ability to rewire connections in areas like the anterior cingulate cortex (responsible for attention) and the fronto-limbic network (responsible for emotional regulation) (Hölzel *et al.* 2011). In a paper analysing the results from multiple studies on the effects of mindfulness in autistic people, the results showed a significant improvement in subjective wellbeing for all participants included (Hartley, Dorstyn, & Due 2019). The practice may be a good way to keep your anxiety levels down, enabling you to feel more in control in social situations and better able to pay attention to the present moment, rather than to fears and negative memories that you may have.

To begin with you could try some simple breathing meditations, which you can practise anywhere you have a few minutes of quiet to yourself. These are also great to do when you start experiencing high levels of distress as part of the distress tolerance exercises.

SIMPLE SOOTHING AND RELAXATION

1. Close your eyes, sit up, and ground your feet so you can feel them touching the floor.
2. Notice your breathing and notice any smells or sounds around you.
3. Take a deep breath and hold it for 10 seconds, let it go and then breath normally. Repeat several times.
4. Starting with your toes and moving up to the top of your head, tense and then relax each muscle in turn.
5. Let any thoughts you have enter, don't fight them away. Just notice them and imagine them passing through your mind, like a train going through the station.

Remember, when doing these exercises, that it's perfectly fine for distracting thoughts to enter your mind. Compassionately watch them float in and out and then refocus your attention on the task.

Gilbert (2009) emphasises not trying to create a state of relaxation, but instead says that relaxation is something that will occur naturally from paying attention to the present moment. If you need a little more help and guidance there are several good meditation and mindfulness apps that might help you (e.g. Headspace), alternatively there may be classes near you or online you can join.

Once you have the hang of this you might want to try introducing some imagery into your mindfulness practices too. Imagined scenes and situations can affect our brains in the same way that experiencing a real scene and situation does (Reddan, Wager, & Schiller 2018). This is why it's so important to find ways to stop dwelling on past negative events and ruminating on potential future adverse events – our brains don't always know these aren't really happening in the present moment (Marchant 2016). By imagining more positive scenarios and environments we can literally recreate the feelings those situations would create in real life, reinforcing neural connections associated with happiness and relaxation (Gilbert 2009). I've outlined a step-by-step meditation I like to do below. I vary in how long I do it for, but usually it is between 5 and 15 minutes long. The first few steps repeat the simple soothing and relaxation meditation above and then go on to include two imagery exercises. The first involves imagining your safe place, somewhere in the past that has made you feel happy and relaxed. I often think of a sunny beach holiday I've been on for this part. Talk yourself through (out loud if it's easier) what the scene looks like, what's happening in the scene, what can you hear and smell, and most importantly how you feel. You can then go on to imagine a scene in the future that you might find stressful, and envisage it going well and you keeping calm in it. Sometimes I imagine going into work for this part, I imagine feeling as relaxed as I did on the beach holiday. I imagine people coming up and talking to me who I don't know, and how calm I remain in these situations that I would in real life find very overwhelming.

The benefit of doing these exercises is that you'll be mentally better prepared for situations in life that increase your anxiety. Rather than being flooded with bad memories and distress when they occur, you can start to feel calmer and the impact they will have on your fight and flight system will be less. We camouflage as a coping mechanism in social situations precisely because of this anxiety and fight or flight system. By hiding our autistic traits we avoid the anxiety that comes with being seen as different or inferior, but in turn this causes us to use vast amounts of energy and increases our future fears of those social situations. Mindfulness is a good way to start calming this system and can prevent us from burning out from our efforts.

IMAGERY RELAXATION

1. Close your eyes, sit up, and ground your feet so you can feel them touching the floor.
2. Notice your breathing and notice any smells or sounds around you.
3. Take a deep breath and hold it for 10 seconds, let it go and then breathe normally. Repeat several times.
4. Starting with your toes and moving up to the top of your head, tense and then relax each muscle in turn.
5. Let any thoughts you have enter, don't fight them away. Just notice them and imagine them passing through your mind, like a train going through the station.
6. Imagine a scene in your head from your past which made you feel happy and relaxed. Talk yourself through that scene and remember how you felt.
7. Now imagine a scene in the future that you might be worried about or that often stresses you out. Imagine feeling as relaxed and calm as you did in the previous scene, and play out in your head this situation going really well.

Seeing the bigger picture

A talent many of us autistic people have is the ability to see the finer details, to notice things others do not. While this is a great skill to have, it's often to the detriment of our ability to see the 'bigger picture'. What this means is that we may focus on the detail and ignore the wider story. For example, I mentioned previously some of the negative thoughts I experienced from one social situation where I bumped into a friend. By only looking at the finer details of this conversation, the fact I forgot to ask her how she was, I ignored the more general experience, which was largely positive. Because of our self-critical thoughts, combined with our natural inclination to focus on details, our focus can often be on the negative. One way we can train our brains to take in the bigger picture is to balance our view with the positives in a situation.

Dr Hamm regularly gets her patients to monitor their lives and record everything that happens in their day. This way when something goes wrong you can reflect on the context or what else happened. Take, for example, a hard day at work when you've come home exhausted and feel like you've achieved nothing. You start to worry about what others will think of you, and you reaffirm all your negative beliefs that you're a failure and not as good as everyone else around you. However, if you looked at the rest of the day, and only compared to yourself and not others, you might see that you actually did incredibly well given what you were up against. Perhaps you didn't sleep very well the night before, you were so busy all day you didn't have time to eat or drink, your boss made some changes at work you weren't expecting, there was a new person in the office, or perhaps you're feeling a little under the weather. All those elements exist outside your control, but could have significantly impacted how you felt and how efficient your performance at work was. Now, if you looked at your diary and saw that despite this exhausting day you'd still managed to cook dinner for yourself, have a bath, and text back your friend, instead of feeling like you'd failed you might instead conclude that actually you managed an awful lot and achieved several positive things too. Ask yourself, given what I've managed to do today and the difficulties I've faced, how well did I do for me? You can keep track in a diary like the one on the following page each day, so whenever you feel like you've failed you have something to look back to and see this in the context of the rest of your day. These kinds of reality checks ensure you stay focused on the bigger picture, rather than hyperfocusing on small, negative details.

★ **Diary of achievements**

Date	What I achieved today	What I struggled with
05/08/22	Managed to start work on time Responded to all my emails Went shopping for food for dinner Cooked, ate, and had time to watch TV after Had a shower Got to bed before 11pm	Lack of sleep from the night before Anxiety about a meeting I have tomorrow My partner is currently away

Another method of focusing on the bigger picture is to practise coming up with three things you're looking forward to every morning and three positives from your day every evening. These don't have to be super exciting and can be as mundane as that you enjoyed dinner or the weather was nice. Some days this is easy and you might have more than three, and other days you might feel like you're really scraping the bottom of the barrel. It's important only to focus on positive things here, and even if you've had a terrible day of anxiety and depression and aren't really feeling anything positive at all, think about things in your day that were objectively positive. For example, you saw a pretty flower, your dog came up to you to be stroked, or you managed to walk to the shops. These don't have to be groundbreaking activities and achievements. My partner and I tend to remind each other each night what our three positives are, but you can also record them in your journal or simply think them to yourself. Remember that all these methods can be adapted to suit you, and if one doesn't help there are many others you can try.

The exercises in this chapter are designed to help you activate your soothing system, turn down your threat system, and to create a more compassionate and less critical self. By doing this your levels of stress and anxiety will lessen and with them your need to focus on your social 'flaws' and perceived failures. As mentioned earlier, the more anxious and depressed you become, the more camouflaging will be used as a coping mechanism. It's important that before you begin practising taking off your mask you're in a good place mentally and are able to be compassionate towards yourself. Even if you do not want to reduce your camouflaging, these exercises will help you to better manage your mental health and reduce the stress you experience in social situations. Some of these exercises you may have found difficult; it's not an easy feat rewiring your thinking patterns and it can take years of practise. If these exercises didn't suit you then there are plenty more you can try; what I've presented here are just some of the ones I have found most useful. What is most important, though, is that you persevere in finding what is right for you, and that you can find a way to be kinder to yourself.

◼ KEY MESSAGES

- Being more compassionate to ourselves means non-judgmentally accepting our feelings.
- Improving our compassion for ourselves helps improve our anxiety and depression, both of which can make us need to camouflage more.
- Many of our automatic thinking patterns contain errors and we cannot take our thoughts as fact.
- Replacing these thoughts with more realistic and positive thoughts can rewire our thinking patterns.
- Sometimes we avoid emotions because they are too distressing, however, this can cause more difficulties long term.
- Practising mindfulness changes connections in areas of the brain that can make us more attentive to the present moment and help us regulate emotions better.
- By looking at the big picture rather than the small details we avoid hyperfocusing on negatives and instead see our difficulties in context.

CHAPTER 5

Taking Off the Mask

> ### CHAPTER'S PURPOSE
> To learn ways of safely testing how it feels to
> purposefully not mask autistic traits and to
> discover new or previous activities that you enjoy
> to learn more about yourself and your identity.

◼ KEY TERMS

- *Cognitive Adaption Model:* The process of adjusting beliefs
  and finding meaning in experiences after a life-threatening
  or traumatic event

In the previous chapters I discussed what camouflaging is, how it
affects us, and ways in which you could reduce the anxiety and depression associated with it. The next step in this journey is to practise
actually taking off the mask and reducing your camouflaging. You
may have got to this point and decided that you don't actually want to
reduce your masking; perhaps it has brought with it many strengths
and helped you more than it has hindered you. This is completely
fine; we are all different and react in different ways, although I would
still encourage you to practise the exercises in the previous chapter
to ensure you're looking after your mental health too. The exercises
outlined in this chapter offer you the chance to test out your unmasking and to rediscover yourself. Maybe there are certain activities and
interests you've stopped doing because you feared what other people
would think of you, or perhaps there are certain social situations

you've found too exhausting to keep up your mask in. The key is to practise unmasking yourself in safe and supportive settings, with people who understand you well. Eventually you might feel confident enough to try some of these exercises in more unfamiliar situations, perhaps with people you don't know or who don't know you as well. However, this comes with a risk of rejection and so needs to be done carefully. Remember, the very reason we have adapted to camouflage in this way is precisely because of this social trauma and fear of rejection and stigmatisation, so it's important that first and foremost we protect ourselves and have compassion for ourselves.

> *Kayleigh described the feeling of not masking as "freeing". She went on to say that it felt "amazing'" to be herself and that she wished she could be that person all the time. In particular she enjoys being able to focus on her special interests and "get overexcited about simple things".*
>
> *Kayleigh went on to explain how she thinks it's important for autistic people to know how common masking is, and that "it takes time to heal from the wounds that made you start masking in the first place, but they will heal". She suggests "[starting] by slowly revealing little parts of your personality that you feel you are masking". She also recommends reaching out to other autistic people, through autism organisations or on social media, describing it as a "warm and welcoming community" that can help support the journey.*

Reconnecting with what makes you happy

After my diagnosis in my early 20s I came to the crashing realisation that I had no idea what I actually enjoyed doing any more. Everything I did seemed to be a tick box of stuff I felt I *should* do. I *should* see that friend. I *should* go to that party. I *should* watch that movie. I *should* read that book. I *should* go on that holiday. Even when I started art therapy to unravel some of these issues, I still felt like I *should* be drawing certain things and in a certain way. When therapists asked me if I actually enjoyed seeing my friends I couldn't honestly answer the question with a "yes". Instead I replied "I guess I do" or "no, but I enjoy knowing I've done it". In a sense I realised my life looked perfect as a series of Instagram posts, but deep down it wasn't exactly what I wanted.

I remember when I first started university and had to pack my bag to move away for the first time in my life. Up until this point I had always slept with a soft toy, as I mentioned previously – a teddy bear made of a silky material that I liked to scratch and feel on my skin. This I now know is called 'stimming', and is a soothing activity many autistic people enjoy. Of course, at the time I was very embarrassed by the enjoyment I got out of what I perceived as a 'childish toy', and so Fred the bear did not come with me to university. I struggled greatly at university. I entered a very deep depression and could often not leave my house. Living with 16 strangers would have been overwhelming for anyone, but for an undiagnosed autistic person it was a living nightmare. I had robbed myself of the one thing that could have helped me with those sleepless nights and been at my side when I felt completely alone, purely because I was ashamed of what my peers would think of me, and because I could not consider that any of them harboured such immature needs. Eventually Fred did get to return to his rightful position in my bed, but only after I'd discovered I was autistic and that depriving myself of something I loved and enjoyed wasn't going to stop me wanting it, and neither was it going to help me cope with the bigger struggles I had in my life. While I once thought I might 'grow out' of this phase of needing a soft toy, I no longer feel the need. In fact, Fred has since disintegrated – only one frazzled ear and mouth remains – but has been replaced by a new, similar silky feeling soft toy.

This is one very specific example of masking, however there are many, many others. Hopefully Chapter 3 highlighted some of the ways you've been hiding your autistic traits, or tried to disguise yourself to 'fit in'. Being diagnosed late makes it tricky to reconnect with your previous self, the self that knew what they liked and enjoyed. Trying to achieve this is also no mean feat. We are essentially building a new identity after years of trying to adapt our identity to please and fit in with others. In a study looking at the experiences of autistic adults diagnosed in later life, we found many of the participants were able to start reframing their identity as a result. However, given how long these participants had lived with their current identity and not known they were autistic, many struggled to view their lives through this new lens (Stagg & Belcher 2019). It's therefore vital that we take baby steps when working on ourselves in this way. As I've done below, start by thinking back to when you last remember being truly happy and yourself, and make a note of the kinds of things you liked doing and which relaxed you.

When do you remember being at your happiest?

Example: Age 12, summer holidays. I had a small circle of close friends, lived at home in a quiet village with my parents, two older brothers, and dog. It was warm out and the evenings were long. Better yet, there was no school.

. . . .

. . . .

. . . .

. . . .

What activities did you like doing?
Example:

- Playing team sports for fun
- Watch kids' TV shows
- Biking around the village all day with my friends
- Playing computer games alone
- Listening to CDs on my Walkman
- Reading teenage fiction books
- Going swimming

. . . .

. . . .

. . . .

. . . .

What things did you do to calm yourself when you felt overwhelmed or upset?

Example:

- ◆ Stroking and scratching with my silky bear
- ◆ Imagining stories in my head
- ◆ Playing with water/being in water

. . . .

. . . .

. . . .

. . . .

Don't worry if you find it too difficult to think of a time you were happy. It's likely that many of us will think back to childhood memories, but for others these memories might be tainted with trauma. It's also important to realise that there may not have been any situations in your life where you feel like you were truly yourself, or that you knew what you enjoyed doing at the time. Likewise, if you do, then these times might have only lasted a very short while, even fleetingly. The situation I gave above covers one summer holiday of my life. I'm sure at the time I was also plagued with the usual anxiety I experienced throughout my childhood, but if I think of when I was most happy this is the first memory I have.

Now, this next part might seem ridiculous, but if you're struggling to work out what you really like and who you really are, try engaging in some of these activities again that once made you happy. We often get accused of immaturity because of our 'childlike' interests, but the reason these activities are so good for us to engage in is precisely because they take us back to that childlike sense of security. Repetitive activities mean doing things we are used to doing and we know we enjoy. In a nutshell, they're safe. When I did this task several years ago I didn't quite feel comfortable enough to join the adult rounders team, but I did open up YouTube and started flicking through some of the old TV programmes I use to like. I also re-downloaded some of my old video games and gave myself dedicated time to just sit and play. No pressures, no rules, just me and something I enjoy. Once I got a bit more confident I joined the gym too so I could use their swimming pool. Not all these activities turned out to be ones I kept up. I soon learned that some of them were better kept in my childhood; for example, teen fiction books weren't quite as exciting as I'd once remembered, and neither was watching repeats of *Sabrina the Teenage Witch*, but I reconnected with an older version of myself that had a better grasp on what the 'less-masked' Hannah use to be like and what she used to enjoy. From there I was able to expand on some of these interests and find new activities that I enjoyed.

Vicky self-identifies as being autistic. She described camouflaging in order to "be taken seriously at work" and also to avoid embarrassing the people around her. This left her "exhausted" and feeling "uneasy" if she felt she hadn't been able to mask well enough. However, she has found relief in being more herself when at home: "[she's] taken to allowing [herself] to spin and dance". She also has found it beneficial to remind herself that her husband and children will love her regardless.

When asked how it feels to not camouflage and what advice she'd give to others, she said that despite feeling nervous about being accepted, she also felt "free, free to be excited, sad...to just feel true joy". She recommends others "use [masking] when you feel you need to, be yourself and avoid it if you don't". Vicky also emphasises the importance of self-care and ensuring masking doesn't impact negatively on wellbeing and mental health like it has for her at times.

The 'soothing and enjoyable activity list' below gives examples of some interests and activities that you might have previously avoided because of how they looked to others, or that you've just become too exhausted to do. Go through each of these and tick any you used to do/would like to do but stopped/don't because of how you feel they would make you appear. Many of these activities are known to be common interests for autistic people because of their soothing and repetitive nature; however, we avoid them in an effort to look less autistic to the outside world. The most obvious of these is stimming. Stimming involves making repetitive movements or noises, and autistic children are often taught to reduce their stims in a bid to appear less autistic. To name just a few, typical examples of stimming include hand flapping, rocking, fiddling with objects, twitching, and vocalisations like muttering and whistling. Of course we now know that appearing less autistic doesn't make someone less autistic and, besides, one cannot become less autistic however much parents/guardians may try (or pay). What was an unconscious behaviour may become more conscious as we grow older and learn to supress these stims as part of our mask. The error has been in thinking autism is a disorder in which stimming behaviours are a symptom. This is incorrect: rather than stimming being a symptom of anything, it is more a coping strategy for autistic people who experience great levels of anxiety trying to fit into environments that aren't adjusted for them. It is often an enjoyable activity that helps regulate sensory input and uncertainty. These thoughts were echoed by a group of autistic adults in a study conducted by Steven Kapp and colleagues (2019) on stimming. They described it as a self-regulatory mechanism to cope with 'overwhelming environments', 'sensory overload', 'noisy thoughts' and 'uncontainable emotion'. These participants also talked of the stigma they faced as a result of their stims, with many supressing stims into more socially acceptable forms like dance or only doing it in private. Last, they spoke of acceptance and the importance of raising understanding in non-autistic people to allow autistic people to stim freely and openly.

My own versions of stims have included scratching silky material, grunting, and twitching parts of my body in symmetry, including my eyebrows, which perpetually makes me look like I'm unhappy with what someone's just said. As I have grown older I have become less concerned by others' reactions to these and more concerned with how they keep me calm in difficult situations. Many autistic and ADHD adults, myself included, have also taken to fidget toys in the last few years to enhance their stimming experience. Fidget toys, such as fidget spinners, tangle toys, and stress balls, have even reached the mainstream with many non-autistic people using them to help their concentration (Farley, Risko, & Kingstone 2013). They're a great way to get back into soothing stimming activities if you're still a little anxious to be seen publicly stimming. Alternatively, I'd suggest trying some of the activities listed here, including stimming, in private first until you build up the confidence to do so more openly.

★ **Soothing and enjoyable activity list**

Activity	Tick if stopped doing or haven't done out of fear *in private*, but would like to	Tick if stopped doing or haven't done out of fear *in public*, but would like to
Playing with fidget toys	☐	☐
Stimming	☐	☐
Singing	☐	☐
Playing an instrument	☐	☐
Listening to music	☐	☐
Dancing	☐	☐
Doing art	☐	☐
Taking photographs	☐	☐
Keeping a scrapbook	☐	☐
Collecting something	☐	☐
Watching children's films or TV	☐	☐
Reading children's books	☐	☐
Playing computer games	☐	☐
Spending time researching/doing a special interest	☐	☐
Petting or playing with an animal	☐	☐
Imagining/fantasising different scenes	☐	☐
Building Lego/other construction toys	☐	☐
Other:	☐	☐
Other:	☐	☐
Other:	☐	☐
Other:	☐	☐

When I was first told I was autistic my biggest confusion was how I could be autistic when I didn't have any special interests or collect anything. It's been somewhat of an autistic stereotype that the old 'male autism' picture painted for us that we are all fascinated by numbers and dates, and of course trainspotting. However, what I realised was that I did have special interests, I'd just been heavily masking these to appear more 'normal'. My obsession with learning everything there was to know about psychology, religions, and other cultures just seemed academic, while my collections of books and soft toys and figurines just seemed mundane. We now know that many autistic people diagnosed as adults have hidden their special interests, or have special interests that can be perceived as 'normal' everyday activities for most people. The difference is in the intensity of these interests and also the comfort they can bring us. Non-autistic people may enjoy their book collections and take pride in them, but that book collection may be a lifesaver for us. It is something to focus on in a world of never-ending uncertainty, it's a safe haven and potentially one of the few things in our lives that brings us real joy and self-worth. Which is exactly why I have included these activities in this book: to encourage you to reconnect with those activities that are just for you and which bring you real joy and comfort. We've spent most of our lives adapting our own interests and activities around those we're with, often neglecting our own needs. To unmask means to start practising being you again – the 'you' that wasn't moulded to fit everyone else's idea of you.

Now you have some idea of the types of activities you used to enjoy – or would like to enjoy – that you've been avoiding, you can begin to implement some of these in your day. Again, take this slowly and try some of these out in private until you gain the confidence to be more open with them in public. Use the diary here to record how they made you feel and whether you'd like to do more of that activity. I've filled in a couple of examples here to get you going.

★ **Monitoring soothing and enjoyable activities**

Activity	How/where I will practise it	What was the outcome? Will I do it again?
Fidget toys	Take my fidget toy to work and use it at my desk to help me stay focused	I felt a bit embarrassed to get it out, but when I did no one seemed to notice it or mention it. It helped me keep calm in a meeting and focus on my work better, so I think I'll keep it on my desk to use in future
Start a collection	I'm going to start collecting figurines from my favourite movies and keeping a database of them	I really enjoyed doing this. It seemed really pointless and a waste of money to start with, but I've been really looking forward to reviewing my database and planning others I want to collect. My Dad did make a comment that it was childish when he saw them, but lots of other adults were buying them in the shop and it makes me feel happy seeing them lined up on my shelf

Remember when practising any of these techniques to continue with the compassion-based activities from the previous chapter. These will help to keep you mindful and to regulate any anxiety or depression you may experience. If someone reacts in a negative or judgemental way towards any of the activities you are practising it is important to remember that they lack insight into your own experiences and needs; put simply, they're ignorant. We could waste a lot of energy explaining to these individuals why they're wrong to judge us, but I would encourage you instead to walk away and remember that you have a large tribe of other autistic folk who think what you're doing is pretty normal and also pretty cool too. Many of these people who judge our activities as immature or pointless are struggling with not having their own needs met. It isn't just autistic people who feel the need to camouflage and pretend to be someone they're not, and it's likely that an element of jealousy is at play here when individuals see others doing something carefree that makes them happy. If you do feel comfortable to explain to others more about your condition then great. If you don't feel ready to do this then it's best to avoid these people, or at least avoid conversations with these people regarding your interests and activities, especially in the early stages of working on yourself and beginning to unmask yourself. It's important we advocate for ourselves and protect ourselves in healthier ways, rather than masking ourselves more to be accepted.

Experimenting with taking off your mask

The final step in this journey is to take everything you have learned about yourself from the exercises in this book and to start applying it to everyday situations. Again, this should be done cautiously and compassionately. There is no rush here. Your camouflage has been built over years and years, and unmasking yourself will likewise be a lengthy journey. My own journey to unmask myself has so far taken since my autism diagnosis was made in 2013 to now, 2021, and is still ongoing. As the years have gone by, and the more work and therapy I have done to reconnect with my true self, the fewer mental health crises I have experienced. What used to occur every six months like clockwork now rears its ugly head every couple of years at most. Of course, there are other factors at play here than just camouflaging, but certainly by reducing my camouflaging I have reduced the amount of stress I experience daily, and that stress can build really fast. I was living like a bucket filled to the brim, which meant any additional stress was enough to tip me right over.

By unmasking I gradually emptied some of that bucket so I could tolerate more stress in other areas of my life. I had more energy to give to other matters and more enjoyable pursuits, including being able to finally write this book.

> Beth described in her email to me how camouflaging makes her feel "fake" and as if she wasn't "showing [her] true self". However, she also felt it was necessary in certain situations for her personal safety, to "not bring attention to [herself], and to pass as neurotypical". She has felt able to attempt to stop camouflaging, however this is predominantly around people she knows well and "knows will accept [her] regardless of how [she] acts". She highlighted the following techniques she has used to attempt to unmask herself:
>
> — reminds herself to just act how she needs to
> — reminds herself that people who around her know her and accept her anyway
> — not berating herself when she messes up socially.

One of the best techniques I learned to achieve this was by using behavioural experiments. This is a common technique used in CBT practice to test out a client's beliefs about themselves and others, and to gather evidence to strengthen new beliefs (Beck *et al.* 1979). The benefit of this technique is that it also gradually exposes you to specific situations you may be fearing, but, rather than flooding yourself, instead you approach the task gradually in a practical and methodical way. Like any good science experiment the task starts with a hypothesis: what do we predict might happen if we don't camouflage in a certain way during a certain situation? Once we've made this prediction we can test it out and see if the awful things we think will happen if we don't camouflage actually do happen, or, even if they do, whether this feels as intolerable to us as we thought it would. This task is a bit more complicated than the others, so let's go through a few examples together. In the following table you can see an example of one of my own behavioural experiments and what the outcome was.

Behavioural experiment example 1

Situation	What do you think will happen?	How will you test this prediction?	What actually happened?	What are your reflections about this prediction?
I'm struggling at work to express the reasonable adjustments I need in place, like having my own desk space and a quiet room I can go to when I feel overwhelmed	If I express my needs at work they'll think I'm difficult and wish they hadn't given me the job, and if other colleagues see I have my own desk and am going off to a quiet room they might think I'm attention seeking	I have a meeting with my manager coming up soon and I can put on the agenda beforehand that I would like to discuss these needs and how they can be met	At first my manager seemed taken aback by what I was telling her and I felt silly for being open with her. However, she went on to thank me for my honesty and said that it would help her better support me. The next day when I was struggling she was able to show me somewhere quiet I could sit, and other colleagues expressed to her too that they admired my honesty and that they enjoyed working with me because of it.	I realised that people can help me more when I'm honest about my needs, and that actually this makes them accept me more, and makes me easier to get on with. It also makes them feel more comfortable and open with me too

In the scenario above my hypothesis was that if I was open about my needs at work, rather than trying to mask them, people would think less of me. My manager would think I was too difficult to work with and my colleagues would think I was attention seeking. I trusted my manager enough to use her in this experiment to find out if this was really true. Her role is to support me and enable me to do my job as well as I possibly can, so she is someone with a vested interest in helping me at work. The outcomes of my experiment were largely positive, and although I did feel silly during the conversation I had with my manager this quickly subsided. In fact, it seemed to help me fit in more that my colleagues and manager knew what I needed and that I was therefore able to be calmer and more myself at work. I could have come out and told my entire team about my needs straight away as part of my experiment, however, I wanted to test out my prediction cautiously and protect myself should it come true. If you would like to try out a similar experiment at work remember to pick someone who you trust first; this could be a fellow colleague who is kind to you if you haven't yet developed a supportive relationship with your manager. Work is a situation in which everyone masks their true selves to some degree, and the nature of being employed often means having to fit in with the organisation's way of behaving. However, this doesn't mean your reasonable adjustments should be ignored, and by adapting the work environment to fit your needs better your employer will get the best out of you, benefiting the whole organisation. Many autistic people struggle to gain and maintain employment. The Office of National Statistics (ONS 2021) recently reported shocking data that only 22 per cent of autistic adults were in any kind of employment. It is unclear why this is, but the most obvious reasons are likely that autistic people face stigma during application and interview processes, and also that many autistic people are unable to work due to co-occurring mental and physical health difficulties. Whether to disclose that you're autistic to your employer, or potential employer, is therefore a difficult decision and one which will depend on individual preferences and circumstances. I have always been open in my job interviews and explained how being autistic gives me many strengths in the workplace. But I must confess that I tend to leave out the reasonable adjustments and needs I have until I've been offered the job and know them a little better.

Once you have a job, though, it's important that you don't use up all your energy and resources every day trying to mask your autism, or you will find yourself completely burnt out in a matter of months. Be strategic in when you need to mask and when actually it's harming you more than it is helping. For example, we all wear a mask in job interviews and try and make a good impression of ourselves, but it's not maintainable to keep this image up five days a week, nine to five. If you struggle in interviews it might be a good idea to conduct a behavioural experiment disclosing to your interviewers that you are autistic and what you may need help with in the interview. I have taken to doing this to try and negate some of the unconscious bias they might have about my atypical social behaviours. I will often tell Human Resources (HR) who organise the interviews that I am autistic, that I may need extra time and details to answer questions accurately, and that meeting new people in new situations exacerbates my anxiety. This may not be a risk you want to take, which is absolutely fine. However, there may be other areas in your life in which you can reduce your camouflaging first. Let's look at a different example.

Behavioural experiment example 2

Situation	What do you think will happen?	How will you test this prediction?	What actually happened?	What are your reflections about this prediction?
I've been invited to a wedding and I'm anxious I won't be able to maintain my mask all day as it's with lots of people I don't know in a new environment	If my mask slips people will think I'm behaving strangely or that I'm not enjoying myself	I will ask a trusted friend/relative from the wedding afterwards how they perceived my behaviour	I explained to a good friend about my behavioural experiment and asked what she thought of my behaviour. She said she hadn't really noticed much as she had been too busy talking with others and trying to keep up appearances herself. Although I seemed quiet at various points she assumed I was just tired as it had been a long day.	People aren't as observant of my behaviours as I think they are. Often people are too busy worrying about their own appearance, or distracted by events around them, that they don't notice. Even when they do notice a change in behaviour, this doesn't mean they judge it negatively.

In the behavioural experiment above you will notice a slightly different approach being used. Rather than testing out behaving in a different way to how I would usually, I instead asked for some feedback on how a close friend had perceived my behaviour. Again, the important part of this test is to choose someone who you can trust to help you. My hypothesis was that if I was around new people in a new environment all day, my mask would slip and people would notice me acting strangely and judge me negatively. What I found instead was that my friend had barely noticed my behaviour as she'd been too busy worrying about hers! While I cannot be sure no one at the wedding judged me negatively, I can be sure that I coped with the situation as best as I could, and my fear of being judged wasn't as great as I expected it to be. We will never be able to control what people think of us, and someone somewhere will always be judging something we do, as we often do to others too. However, often our anticipation of that judgement is greater than the reality. The more experiments like the one above you practise, the more evidence you will gather that, on the whole, our beliefs about what others will think of us are often exaggerated and based on 'worst-case scenarios'. Ultimately, it comes down to asking yourself the question, how much does it matter if someone judges me negatively? What is the worst that will come from that judgement? Often the answer is that it will feel really unpleasant for a while and that we might feel really silly. If this is the case then I would recommend returning to the 'distress tolerance' exercises in the previous chapter, and working through practising managing these uncomfortable feelings. Of course, others' judgement can also have some more serious consequences. When this turns to bullying or discrimination then action needs to be taken to prevent that individual from causing more harm. If this is something you think you're currently experiencing then avoid opening yourself up with these behavioural experiences to those people, remove yourself from those situations where possible, and instead reach out to someone who can give you support. Remember, while this book is about you taking control and changing your own approach in some situations, that doesn't mean we have to tolerate the bad behaviour of others while they take no responsibility for how their actions make us feel. Let's explore another example.

Behavioural experiment example 3

Situation	What do you think will happen?	How will you test this prediction?	What actually happened?	What are your reflections about this prediction?
My friend has asked me to go to a concert at the weekend but I really don't like the band or feel I can cope with the busy venue	If I tell her I don't want to come she will feel let down, that I'm boring, and won't ask me to do things again	I can send her a text and explain that while I enjoy spending time with her I don't feel able to make the concert this weekend as I've had a busy week and it's not really my kind of music	Once I sent the text I felt so anxious and kept checking my phone for her reply. When she text back she just said that was fine and not to worry. I was worried she was annoyed with me and being 'off' but she text later asking if I just wanted to grab some food and watch a film at the weekend instead.	People won't think I'm boring just because I don't like something they do, and they will still want to spend time with me doing something we both enjoy doing. Also, by saying 'no' this time it means I've set a boundary that I don't have to say 'yes' to everything I get asked to do, and people won't think less of me.

This third example illustrates a common situation I find myself in, being asked to do something I don't want to do and not feeling like I can say no. Part of my camouflage is to appear likeable and agreeable to everyone, and saying no conflicts with this core belief that I must always say yes. I predict here that by saying I don't want to go to a concert with my friend she will then think badly of me and may not want to do other things with me in the future. Many of these beliefs reflect the thinking errors that were discussed in the last chapter; for example, I'm fortune telling how my friend will react, blowing things out of proportion by assuming this will affect our future, and mind reading that she will think badly of me. Instead what this experiment showed was that my friend respected my choice, as I would have done hers, and still values our friendship and the time we spend together. Ultimately, no one wants to be hanging out with someone who is forcing themselves to be there, and my friend would have probably been upset to learn I had said yes to attending the concert with her when I didn't like the music or being in the venue. Now she won't ask me to go to a concert like that again, and she has a better idea of the things I do like – watching films and eating food! Feeling the need to have the same interests as our peers and 'following the crowd' is pretty common as we are growing up. Many of us spent our teenage years struggling to keep up with the next 'in thing' and keeping ahead with fashion. I vividly remember times when I slipped up, getting the new 'must have' toy a few months too late when it was no longer in favour, or expressing interest for some very uncool hobby that was most definitely not shared by any of my peers (e.g World War II evacuees, watercolour paintings of churches, and practising non-fiction writing, to name but a few). The embarrassment and exposure I felt from this motivated me to hide my true interests, likes, and dislikes, and instead follow what everyone else was doing. However, as I explained in Chapter 2, this strategy may have worked as we were growing up, but is no longer needed in adulthood. In adulthood individuality is celebrated more, and we tend to appreciate people who stand out from the crowd and know their own minds well, rather than those who just follow the crowd. These behavioural experiments are a good way for you to start practising expressing your own individuality more as an autistic adult. Let's look at one last example.

Behavioural experiment example 4

Situation	What do you think will happen?	How will you test this prediction?	What actually happened?	What are your reflections about this prediction?
I always have to try really hard to stop myself flicking my fingers (stimming) in public	If people see me doing this they will think there is something wrong with me and that I'm 'crazy'	I'm going to let myself flick my fingers for a few seconds while I'm on the train	I was a bit nervous at first but the train was empty, and I started by hiding my flicking under my jumper. Eventually I did it more in the open. Someone looked at me but then just looked away. I didn't notice anyone laughing or talking about me.	It's difficult to know what people on the train were thinking, but it felt quite liberating and calming to stim freely. I would like to test this more in busier places.

This last experiment is a trickier one to test. I predicted that if I stimmed in public, by flicking my fingers, others would laugh at me or think something was wrong with me. I can't know what other people did think of this, but nothing awful happened to me as a result of doing this in public. I could test this out further in a more crowded setting, or I could ask someone I'm with what they think about me doing it.

Now it's your turn to try out your own behavioural experiments. When trying to think of potential behavioural experiments look back on the camouflaging behaviours you identified earlier in Chapter 3 and think of specific scenarios where you could test reducing some of these out. Remember to look at ways you mask your autistic traits, ways you compensate for your autistic traits, as well as ways you just generally try to 'fit in' more. I would recommend thinking up situations and experiments that are more personal to you. Remember to be specific and to carefully choose settings in which you can test them out safely. Some of your behavioural experiments may be short-term experiments; that is, they're meant to test whether your predictions come true or whether your fears aren't actually realised. I wouldn't suggest always purposefully doing these in every social interaction you have, or you will find it as exhausting as masking. You can just try them out a few times and see if you really need to be as conscious of camouflaging in this way as you think you do. You can base your findings on how doing the experiments made you feel. Were you more relaxed? Did it make the conversation easier to follow? Did you have more energy afterwards? Or you can do them with someone close to you and ask them how they perceived your behaviour. Did they find you or your behaviour 'odd'? Did they notice what you were doing? What were their impressions of the social interaction in general?

★ Practice behavioural experiments

Situation	What do you think will happen?	How will you test this prediction?	What actually happened?	What are your reflections about this prediction?

Many of our camouflaging behaviours are too ingrained and automatic to test out with behavioural experiments, for example wanting to fit in and mirroring others' facial expressions and body postures. However, the more you practise reducing the ones conscious to you that are using up lots of your energy, the more your anxiety in these situations will hopefully reduce too. I will reiterate here that you don't have to stop camouflaging; the point of these exercises is to work out actually how much stress it's causing you and whether there are any techniques you can use that will reduce this. You might find that opening up to people close to you and asserting your wants and needs more helps in itself. Also, you might find the compassion-based mindfulness exercises on the previous pages are enough. The key here is to put yourself first rather than considering how others will think of you, which is historically what we've been spending most of our lives doing. As I mentioned at the start of this book, sometimes doing these kinds of self-help exercises can trigger negative feelings. If at any point you find your anxiety levels increase or your mood dipping, take a break from them and do something relaxing you enjoy. If when you return to the exercise you find it too stressful again, skip to the next one; you can always come back to these exercises when you're ready.

Rebuilding your self

One of the biggest challenges in this process is rediscovering areas of our lives where we haven't been happy, or where we haven't been able to be our true selves. Some of us will have had awareness of our camouflaging and difficulties, while others of us may not have been as aware. Especially if you received your autism diagnosis late, it is likely that you have been through quite an emotional rollercoaster of coming to terms with this. We have to reconcile our 'old self' with our new 'future self'. The Cognitive Adaption Model, first proposed by Taylor (1983), explains how gaining new life-changing information about ourselves requires us to re-evaluate our sense of self and our future identities. The three steps to achieving this are: (1) finding meaning in the experience; (2) regaining control over the event and one's life; and (3) enhancing our self-esteem. In the first part of this book we looked at step 1, the meaning behind our experiences. By better understanding coping mechanisms we developed, like camouflaging, and why we developed them, we can understand our experiences in a more meaningful way. It's easy to catastrophise and think your whole life has therefore been a lie; but this is another thinking error and will only lead to depression and despair. A more realistic summary is that your life has not been a lie; you have always been you but certain difficulties in your environment have made it harder for you to express that self. It is likely that many positive things have also happened along your journey and that you have grown in strength as a result, although this might be a little hard for you to see right now. The second step, regaining control, can be achieved by working on the exercises in this book. This involves refocusing on your beliefs and altering your thinking errors by instilling more compassionate thoughts, as well as practising activities that you enjoy while saying no to those you don't want to partake in any more. In the final section of this chapter we will turn to the last of these three steps: enhancing self-esteem. Hopefully reading the snippets taken from others' experiences throughout this book has made you realise that you are not alone, and that many others are currently sharing similar experiences to you. This is a good place to start when it comes to boosting your own self-esteem and gaining confidence to express yourself more. The next exercise looks at how to determine what your values and goals are, and how you can harness these to enhance your feelings of self-worth.

This first exercise is designed to get you thinking about what your core values might be, by reviewing what you admire about other people in your life. I've given some examples of who these people might be and what their values might look like. Don't worry if you can't think of anyone in your life who fits into these brackets, or that you just don't admire very much! You can also reflect on people from your past too, or people you don't know personally.

★ **People I admire**

Area of your life	Person	What I admire most about them
Family	*Example:* James (brother)	*Example:* Laid back and doesn't get angry with people
Partner	*Example:* Megan (wife)	*Example:* Patient and forgiving
Friend	*Example:* Allie	*Example:* Compassionate and understanding of others' beliefs and experiences
Work colleague		
Teacher		
Celebrity		
Doctor		
Therapist/support worker		
In your community		
Other:		

Looking at the values that you most admire in these people, which do you consider to be the most important? List a couple of these in the table below and consider scenarios where you have demonstrated that quality, and future scenarios where you can practise them more.

★ **Examples of values I admire**

Value	Past example	Future example
Example: Compassion	I had an argument with my partner where I felt I was in the right, however I saw that she was really upset and so put my feelings aside to comfort her and listen to her side	Next time someone does something that makes me angry, I'm going to stop and first try and understand where they're coming from and why they might have acted in that way

The purpose of this exercise isn't to force yourself into being more virtuous based on others' ideals; rather, the idea is to focus on things you personally value. For example, many people value others speaking their mind. Objectively this seems like a good value to have; however, I personally wouldn't list this as an important value for myself. I much more admire people who are compassionate and who can respond with empathy regardless of their own feelings. Neither approach is right or wrong, it's just a matter of personal experience and preference. This is why the first exercise honed in on specific people's values, to help you gauge better what is most important to you. It is likely that because these values are important to you, they'll make you feel especially good about yourself when you practise them, which in turn will help you build your confidence and self-worth. By camouflaging you may have had to bury some of these values in order to focus on how others want you to act.

The last chapter worked on your self-confidence and self-compassion, but the exercises in this chapter are designed to help you apply what you've learned about yourself and your masking in real-life situations. By camouflaging and continually living in that cycle of stress and anxiety you leave very little time to do the things you enjoy and develop your own interests. You may find you spend most of your energy practising and rehearsing social situations to ensure others' approval. By practising the gentle exercises in this chapter you can gradually release the pressure valve on your stress and start prioritising more time to rediscover yourself. I personally found some of these exercises quite difficult. After spending years trying to avoid any uncomfortable feelings caused by upsetting others or bringing attention to myself, doing the opposite and testing myself around others was terrifying. The key to my success was to take these steps slowly, with people I trusted, and to keep a record of my progress. By doing this I was able to gauge how much of my masking I was able to give up and how much I still needed, or that wasn't worth the stress of trying to stop at this current point in my life. You may decide you don't want to stop any of it, or even that you want to mask more; the important factor here is that you are making a decision for you and only you, and that you've reached that decision through developing stronger self-awareness and compassion.

KEY MESSAGES

- Camouflaging can use up your energy, leaving you less time to do the things you enjoy or that make you 'you'.
- Re-engage with activities you used to enjoy but have stopped doing, or that you've had less time to do.
- Practise gentle ways of unmasking yourself to people you know. Record how it goes and plan future 'experiments'.
- Focus on what you like about others and what your key values are. By aligning your actions and behaviours more to these values you are reinforcing positive thoughts about yourself, and reducing those anxious ones that might be making you feel inadequate.

CHAPTER 6

Final Thoughts

I started writing this book straight after finishing my PhD at the end of 2019, just as the world was about to be thrown into chaos by the Covid-19 pandemic. I wanted to share my own therapeutic experiences, as well as the knowledge I'd gained from studying autistic camouflaging, to help others less fortunate than myself to have access to the kind of information and mental health support I had. I would not be where I am today without the invaluable input from professionals who helped me to identify my own camouflaging and to explore ways of discovering my 'true self' again. Many of us with late diagnoses have years of camouflaging to work through to get to this point. We carry it with us like a thick fog we can never quite see through. In truth, finally receiving the autism diagnosis is only one small part of the picture in learning about ourselves. It helps us to realise a lost part of our identity, but no one then explains how we can overcome years of trauma and not knowing.

At the beginning of this book I said I had felt I had reached the top of the mountain on my journey to rediscovering who I am post diagnosis. However, this was not quite true. Being forced into lockdown while writing this book allowed me to see how much of my life was still spent camouflaging. Suddenly not having to go to work every day and meet people, or going out socialising multiple times a week, I realised how exhausted I still was. So as I wrote this book I also worked through these exercises again myself. I think it's safe to say that my mission to reduce my camouflaging will always be a balancing act I need to work on. As I learned from the people I spoke to while writing this book, many of us still need to camouflage to cope with our lives and to feel confident around others.

However, almost everyone said they had been exhausted by doing it, and the most common piece of advice given was to try and find regular time where you don't need to camouflage and you can relax. So this became the main aim of the book. Not to tell autistic people to stop camouflaging and to go unleash their true autistic selves, but to know yourself better and learn better ways to manage that exhaustion. Essentially to create more safe and compassionate spaces to be able to sometimes take off that mask.

As I finished my PhD and began writing this book a debate emerged within the autistic community around the whole concept of camouflaging. Some argued that it wasn't a feature of autism but a feature of all human behaviour, and others felt it unfairly placed blamed on the autistic person for intentionally concealing traits and acting in a different way. I hope I've been clear in this book that while all humans do copy and mimic others to learn, for those who feel disconnected from society because their behaviours are deemed 'atypical', this mimicking can be much more intense. So while a non-autistic person may camouflage certain aspects of themselves, most don't need to hide all their natural behaviours, and certainly not as intensely or for as long. It is this intensity and length of time that causes exhaustion and the eventual 'burn out'. Similarly, I hope I've also been clear in this book that camouflaging is not the fault of the person using it. These behaviours start unconsciously from a young age as a response to social traumas and serve to protect an individual well into adulthood. We might become aware of camouflaging as a coping mechanism in adulthood, but it is a reaction of our past experiences as children. What really needs to change is the stigma that is associated with 'being different', but this will not happen overnight, and until then we must protect ourselves and prioritise our own wellbeing as much as we can.

As I have mentioned throughout this book, some of these tools and tips you may find too hard, or some you may find completely useless, and that's OK. We all have different needs and abilities, which is what makes trying to find a universal approach that helps all autistic people impossible. I am well aware that this book only serves those of us without severe intellectual disabilities; however, camouflaging and mental health difficulties are not limited to those of us who have insight into our condition. This is why those of us who can speak out and share our experiences are key to making sure our community and our needs are heard. We are all so different, yet face many of the same daily battles and challenges.

Compassion for ourselves and our fellow autistic friends is crucial. The likelihood is that you've grown up in a society that has constantly tried to change you and told you that your behaviour is not 'appropriate' or not 'the norm'. This may have been quite subtle, or you may have experienced it as a slap in the face wherever you've turned and no matter how hard you've tried. Living with this stigma and 'difference' day in and day out takes its toll. We may not even realise just how much, but constantly trying to adapt and change ourselves to 'fit in' will lead to high levels of self-criticism and shame about who we are. Perhaps, like me, you've been doing this so long you don't even really know who you are in the first place. As adults we now have a choice to begin to unravel some of that shame and try and work backwards to rediscover our identities and who we want to be. But we have to be kind to ourselves and not beat ourselves up about who we've become. We experience enough criticism from others that the very least we can do is to give ourselves the break we so desperately need. There is nothing wrong with you, and there are thousands of other people out there just like you.

I hope at the very least that you will find in this book stories just like yours, so that you feel less alone in your journey. Becoming more aware of ourselves so that we can better advocate for ourselves is the first step in recovering from years' worth of ostracism and social trauma. Having the confidence to say 'no' to people, and not feeling bad about doing so, and having the ability to stand up for our own needs, without being criticised, is an incredibly freeing feeling. I have spoken to people, diagnosed in their 50s, who have decided to completely unmask themselves and free themselves of their camouflaging behaviours, but I have also spoke to people who don't want to give these up because they help them to feel confident and they like who they are when they use them. The key is having the choice, but we can only make that choice when we have all the information and are fully aware of ourselves.

If you are a parent/guardian of an autistic child, or someone working with an autistic person, I hope this book will provide some answers as to why they might be struggling with exhaustion and/or their mental health. There are of course other reasons too why this might be happening, but in my experience camouflaging and feeling pressured to 'fit in' is often the main culprit. Being a safe person with whom that individual can feel comfortable enough around to not need to mask could make a huge difference, not only to their current wellbeing but also to their long-term mental health. By feeding into the narrative that there is something different about them that means they must adapt to be accepted by others, you are adding to their already over-spilling bucket of self-critical thoughts. So I encourage you to be that person in their life that says it's OK for them to flap their hands in front of you, to talk about whatever interests them until they run out of air, to stare into empty space while you're asking them questions, or to just sit quietly and not need to say anything at all. Focus on what brings them joy and comfort, rather than what they cannot or find too difficult to do. And most importantly, reinforce that they are likeable and accepted for who they are.

At the heart of the issue is belonging. It is a universal human need and one that almost all of us struggle to find at times. In my opinion there is no greater feeling than feeling like you are a person who belongs where you are with those around you, no greater feeling still than belonging in that place as your full, true self. This is why it is so important that we are able to find and carve out these spaces, to give ourselves the respite we so desperately need in our lives to truly relax.

References

Asendorpf, J. B. (2002). Self-awareness, other-awareness, and secondary representation. In A. N. Meltzoff & W. Prinz (eds) *The Imitative Mind: Development, Evolution, and Brain Bases* (pp. 63–73). Cambridge: Cambridge University Press.

Ashworth, F., Clarke, A., Jones, L., Jennings, C., & Longworth, C. (2014). An exploration of compassion focused therapy following acquired brain injury. *Psychology and Psychotherapy: Theory, Research and Practice*, 88(2), 143–162. doi: 10.1111/papt.12037

Attwood, T. (2006). *The Complete Guide to Asperger's Syndrome*. London: Jessica Kingsley Publishers.

Bagatell, N. (2007). Orchestrating voices: autism, identity and the power of discourse. *Disability & Society*, 4, 413–426. doi: 10.1080/09687590701337967

Bailenson, J. N., & Yee, N. (2005). Digital chameleons: automatic assimilation of nonverbal gestures in immersive virtual environments. *Psychological Science*, 16(10), 814–819. doi: 10.1111/j.1467-9280.2005.01619.x

Baldwin, S., & Costley, D. (2016). The experiences and needs of female adults with high-functioning autism spectrum disorder. *Autism*, 20(4), 483–495. doi: 10.1177/1362361315590805

Baron-Cohen, S. (2012). *The Extreme Male-Brain Theory of Autism*. London: Penguin.

Baron-Cohen, S., Richler, J., Bisarya, D., Gurunathan, N., & Wheelwright, S. (2003). The systemising quotient: an investigation of adults with Asperger syndrome or high-functioning autism, and normal sex differences. *Philosophical Transactions of the Royal Society B: Biological Sciences*, 538(1430), 361–374. doi: 10.1098/rstb.2002.1206

Beck, A. T., Rush, A. J., Shaw, B. F., & Emery, G. (1979). *Cognitive Therapy of Depression*. New York: Guilford Press.

Beck, J. S. (2011). *Cognitive Behavior Therapy: Basics and Beyond* (2nd ed.). New York: Guilford Press.

Belcher, H. L., Morein-Zamir, S., Mandy, W., & Ford, R. M. (2021). Camouflaging intent, first impressions, and age of ASC diagnosis in autistic men and women. *Journal of Autism and Developmental Disorders*, Advance online publication. doi: 10.1007/s10803-021-05221-3

Bellebaum, C., & Daum, I. (2007). Cerebellar involvement in executive control. *Cerebellum*, 6(3), 184–192. doi: 10.1080/14734220601169707

Bem, S. L. (1981). Gender schema theory: a cognitive account of sex typing. *Psychological Review*, 88(4), 354–364. doi: 10.1037/0033-295X.88.4.354

Bird, G., & Viding, E. (2014). The self to other model of empathy: providing a new framework for understanding empathy impairments in psychopathy, autism, and alexithymia. *Neuroscience & Biobehavioral Reviews*, 47, 520–532. doi: 10.1016/j.neubiorev.2014.09.021.

Bölte, S., Duketis, E., Poustka, F., & Holtmann, M. (2011) Sex differences in cognitive domains and their clinical correlates in higher-functioning autism spectrum disorders. *Autism*, 5(4), 497–511. doi: 10.1177/1362361310391116

Bundy, R., Mandy, W., Crane, L., Belcher, H., *et al.* (2021, February 2). The impact of COVID-19 on the mental health of autistic adults in the UK: a mixed-methods study. *OSF Preprints*. doi: 10.31219/osf.io/9v5qh

Cage, E., & Troxell-Whitman, Z. (2019). Understanding the reasons, contexts and costs of camouflaging for autistic adults. *Journal of Autism and Developmental Disorders*, 49(5), 1899–1911. doi: 10.1007/s10803-018-03878-x

Carpenter, M. (2006). Instrumental, social, and shared goals and intentions in imitation. In S. J. Rogers & J. H. G. Willams (eds) *Imitation and the Social Mind: Autism and Typical Development* (pp. 48–70). New York: Guilford Press.

Cassidy, S., Bradley, L., Shaw, R., & Baron-Cohen, S. (2018). Risk markers for suicidality in autistic adults. *Molecular Autism,* 9(42), 1–14. doi: 10.17863/CAM.33147

Chartrand, T. L., & Bargh, J. A. (1999). The chameleon effect: the perception–behavior link and social interaction. *Journal of Personality and Social Psychology*, 76(6), 893–910. doi: 10.1037/0022-3514.76.6.893

Cooper, K., Smith, L. G. E., & Russell, A. (2017). Social identity, self-esteem, and mental health in autism. *European Journal of Social Psychology*, 47(7), 844–854. doi: 10.1002/ejsp.2297

Dean, M., Harwood, R., & Kasari, C. (2017). The art of camouflage: gender differences in the social behaviors of girls and boys with autism spectrum disorder. *Autism*, 21(6), 678–689. doi: 10.1177/1362361316671845

Ellis, A. (1957). Rational psychotherapy and individual psychology. *Journal of Individual Psychology*, 13(1), 38–44.

Estow, S., Jamieson, P., & Yates, J.R. (2006). Self-monitoring and mimicry of positive and negative social behaviours. *Journal of Research in Personality*, 41(2), 425–433. doi: 10.1016/j.jrp.2006.05.003

Farley, J., Risko, E. F., & Kingstone, A. (2013). Everyday attention and lecture retention: the effects of time, fidgeting, and mind wandering. *Frontiers in Psychology*, 4, 619. doi: 10.3389/fpsyg.2013.00619

Fine, C. (2010). *Delusions of Gender: How Our Minds, Society, and Neurosexism Create Difference* (1st ed.). New York: W. W. Norton.

Freud, S. (1962). *The Ego and the Id: (Complete Psychological Works of Sigmund Freud).* New York: Norton.

Gilbert, P. (2009). *The Compassionate Mind.* London: Robinson.

Goffman, E. (1990). *The Presentation of Self in Everyday Life.* London: Penguin.

Greenberger, D., & Padesky, C. A. (2016). *Mind Over Mood* (2nd ed.). New York: Guilford Press.

Harari, Y. N. (2014). *Sapiens: A Brief History of Humankind.* London: Vintage.

Hartley, M., Dorstyn, D., & Due, C. (2019). Mindfulness for children and adults with autism spectrum disorder and their caregivers: a meta-analysis. *Journal of Autism and Developmental Disorders*, 49, 4306–4319. doi: 10.1007/s10803-019-04145-3

Hayes, S. C., Strosahl, K. D., & Wilson, K. G. (2012). *Acceptance and Commitment Therapy: The Process and Practice of Mindful Change* (2nd ed.). New York: Guilford Press.

Hendrickx, S. (2015). *Women and Girls with Autism Spectrum Disorder: Understanding Life Experiences from Early Childhood to Old Age*. London: Jessica Kingsley Publishers.

Hollocks, M. J., Lerh, J. W., Magiati, I., Meiser-Stedman, R., & Brugha, T. S. (2019). Anxiety and depression in adults with autism spectrum disorder: a systematic review and meta-analysis. *Psychological Medicine*, 49(4), 559–572. doi: 10.1017/S0033291718002283

Hölzel, B. K., Lazar, S. W., Gard. T., Schuman-Olivier, Z., Vago, D. R., & Ott, U. (2011). How does mindfulness meditation work? Proposing mechanisms of action from a conceptual and neural perspective. *Perspectives on Psychological Science*, 6(6), 537–559. doi: 10.1177/1745691611419671

Hull, L., Lai, M.-C., Baron-Cohen, S., Allison, C., *et al.* (2020). Gender differences in self-reported camouflaging in autistic and non-autistic adults. *Autism: The International Journal of Research and Practice*, 24(2), 252–263. doi: 10.1177/1362361319864804

Hull, L., Mandy, W., Lai, M.-C., Baron-Cohen, S., *et al.* (2019). Development and validation of the Camouflaging Autistic Traits Questionnaire (CAT-Q). *Journal of Autism and Developmental Disorders*, 49(3), 819–833. doi: 10.1007/s10803-018-3792-6

Hull, L., Petrides, K. V., Allison, C., Smith, P., *et al.* (2017). "Putting on my best normal": social camouflaging in adults with autism spectrum conditions. *Journal of Autism and Developmental Disorders*, 47(8), 2519–2534. doi: 10.1007/s10803-017-3166-5

Ickes, W., Holloway, R., Stinson, L. L., & Hoodenpyle, T. G. (2006). Self-monitoring in social interaction: the centrality of self-affect. *Journal of Personality*, 74(3), 659–684. doi: 10.1111/j.1467-6494.2006.00388.x

Kapp, S. K., Steward, R., Crane, L., Elliott, D., *et al.* (2019). "People should be allowed to do what they like": autistic adults' views and experiences of stimming. *Autism*, 23(7), 1782–1792. doi: 10.1177/1362361319829628

Klimecki, O. M., Leiberg, S., Lamm, C., & Singer, T. (2013). Functional neural plasticity and associated changes in positive affect after compassion training. *Cerebral Cortex*, 23(7), 1552–1561. doi: 10.1093/cercor/bhs142

Kopp, S., & Gillberg, C. (1992). Girls with social deficits and learning problems: autism, atypical Asperger syndrome or a variant of these conditions. *European Child & Adolescent Psychiatry*, 1(2), 89–99. doi: 10.1007/BF02091791

Lai, M.-C., Lombardo, M. V., Ruigrok, A. N. V., Chakrabarti, B., *et al.* (2012). Cognition in males and females with autism: similarities and differences. *PLoS ONE*, 7(10). doi: 10.1371/journal.pone.0047198

Lai, M.-C., Lombardo, M. V., Ruigrok, A. N., Chakrabarti, B., *et al.* (2017). Quantifying and exploring camouflaging in men and women with autism. *Autism*, 21(6), 690–702. doi: 10.1177/1362361316671012

Lawson, W. B. (2020). Adaptive morphing and coping with social threat in autism: an autistic perspective. *Journal of Intellectual Disability Diagnosis and Treatment*, 8(8), 519–526. doi: 10.6000/2292-2598.2020.08.03.29

Leith, K. P., & Baumeister, R. (2008). Empathy, shame, guilt, and narratives of interpersonal conflicts: guilt-prone people are better at perspective taking. *Journal of Personality*, 66(1), 1–37. doi: 10.1111/1467-6494.00001

Linehan, M. M., Armstrong, H. E., Suarez, A., Allmon, D., & Heard, H. L. (1991). Cognitive-behavioral treatment of chronically parasuicidal borderline patients. *Archives of General Psychiatry*, 48(12), 1060–1064. doi: 10.1001/archpsyc.1991.01810360024003

Little, L. (2002). Middle-class mother's perceptions of peer and sibling victimisation among children with Asperger's syndrome and nonverbal learning disorders. *Issues in Comprehensive Pediatric Nursing*, 25, 43–57. doi: 10.1080/014608602753504847

Livingston, L. A., & Happé, F. (2017). Conceptualising compensation in neurodevelopmental disorders: reflections from autism spectrum disorder. *Neuroscience & Biobehavioral Reviews*, 80, 729–742. doi: 10.1016/j.neubiorev.2017.06.005

Livingston, L. A., Colvert, E., Bolton, P., & Happé, F. (2018). Good social skills despite poor theory of mind: exploring compensation in autism spectrum disorder. *Journal of Child Psychology and Psychiatry*, 60(1), 102–110. doi: 10.1111/jcpp.12886

Mandy, W. (2019). Social camouflaging in autism: is it time to lose the mask? *Autism*, 23(8), 1879–1881. doi: 10.1177/1362361319878559

Mandy, W., Chilvers, R., Chowdhury, U., Salter, G., Seigal, A., & Skuse, D. (2012). Sex differences in autism spectrum disorder: evidence from a large sample of children and adolescents. *Journal of Autism and Developmental Disorders*, 42(7), 1304–1313. doi: 10.1007/s10803-011-1356-0

Marchant, J. (2016). *Cure: A Journey into the Science of Mind Over Body.* New York: Crown Publishing Group.

McGuigan, N., Makinson, J., & Whiten, A. (2011). From over-imitation to super-copying: adults imitate causally irrelevant aspects of tool use with higher fidelity than young children. *British Journal of Psychology*, 102(1), 1–18. doi: 10.1348/000712610X493115

Meltzoff, A. N. (1995). Understanding the intentions of others: re-enactment of intended acts by 18-month-old children. *Developmental Psychology*, 31(5), 838–850. doi: 10.1037/0012-1649.31.5.838

Meltzoff, A. N. (2002). Elements of a developmental theory of imitation. In A. N. Meltzoff & W. Prinz (eds) *The Imitative Mind: Development, Evolution, and Brain Bases* (pp. 19–41). Cambridge: Cambridge University Press.

Milton, D. E. M. (2012). On the ontological status of autism: the double empathy problem. *Disability & Society*, 27(6), 883–887. doi: 10.1080/09687599.2012.710008

Mishima, Y. (2017). *Confessions of a Mask.* London: Penguin.

Morrison, K. E., DeBrabander, K. M., Jones, D. R., Faso, D. J., Ackerman, R. A., & Sasson, N. J. (2020). Outcomes of real-world social interaction for autistic adults paired with autistic compared to typically developing partners. *Autism*, 24(5), 1067–1080. doi: 10.1177/1362361319892701

Nadel, J. (2002). Imitation and imitation recognition: functional use in preverbal infants and nonverbal children with autism. In A. N. Meltzoff & W. Prinz (eds) *The Imitative Mind: Development, Evolution, and Brain Bases* (pp. 42–62). Cambridge: Cambridge University Press.

NAS (2016). The autism employment gap: too much information in the workplace. Accessed on 27/1/22 at https://s3.chorus-mk.thirdlight.com/file/1573224908/64036150693/width=-1/height=-1/format=-1/fit=scale/t=445570/e=never/k=b0347eba/TMI-Employment-Report-24pp-WEB-291020.pdf

ONS (2021). Outcomes for disabled people in the UK: 2020. Accessed on 27/1/22 at www.ons.gov.uk/peoplepopulationandcommunity/healthandsocialcare/disability/articles/outcomesfordisabledpeopleintheuk/2020

Otterman, D.L., Koopman-Verhoeff, M.E., White, T.J., Tiemeier, H. *et al.* (2019). Executive functioning and neurodevelopmental disorders in early childhood: a prospective population-based study. *Child and Adolescent Psychiatry and Mental Health*, 13, art. 38. doi: 10.1186/s13034-019-0299-7

Pelton, M. K., & Cassidy, S. A. (2017). Are autistic traits associated with suicidality? A test of the interpersonal-psychological theory of suicide in a non-clinical young adult sample. *Autism Research*, 10(11), 1891–1904. doi: 10.1002/aur.1828

Pennington, B. F., & Ozonoff, S. (1996). Executive functions and developmental psychopathology. *Journal of Child Psychology and Psychiatry*, 37(1), 51–87. doi: 10.1111/j.1469-7610.1996.tb01380.x

Piaget, J. (1972). *Psychology of the Child*. New York: Basic Books.

Reddan, M. C., Wager, T. D., & Schiller, D. (2018). Attenuating neural threat expression with imagination. *Neuron*, 100(4), 994–1005. doi: 10.1016/j.neuron.2018.10.047

Sasson, N. (2021, March 1). *Interpersonal Mechanisms of Social Disability Seminar* [Lecture recording at Durham University]. Accessed on 27/1/22 at www.youtube.com/watch?v=elMeUjMr7GY

Sasson, N. J., & Morrison, K. E. (2019). First impressions of adults with autism improve with diagnostic disclosure and increased autism knowledge of peers. *Autism*, 23(1), 50–59. doi: 101177%2F1362361317729526

Sasson, N. J., Faso, D. J., Nugent, J., Lovell, S., Kennedy, D. P., & Grossman, R. B. (2017). Neurotypical peers are less willing to interact with those with autism based on thin slice judgments. *Scientific Reports*, 7(1), 40700–40700. doi: 10.1038/srep40700

Sedgewick, F., Hull, L., & Ellis, H. (2021). *Autism and Masking: How and Why People Do It, and the Impact It Can Have*. London: Jessica Kingsley Publishers.

Sedgewick, F., Hill, V., Yates, R., Pickering, L., & Pellicano, E. (2016). Gender differences in the social motivation and friendship experiences of autistic and non-autistic adolescents. *Journal of Autism and Developmental Disorders*, 46(4), 1297–1306. doi: 10.1007/s10803-015-2669-1

Shonin, E., Van Gordon, W., Compare, A., Zangeneh, M. & Griffiths, M.D. (2015). Buddhist-derived loving-kindness and compassion meditation for the treatment of psychopathology: a systematic review. *Mindfulness*, 6, 1161–1180. doi: 10.1007/s12671-014-0368-1

Silberman, S. (2017). *Neurotribes: The Legacy of Autism and How to Think Smarter About People Who Think Differently*. Sydney: Allen & Unwin.

Solomon, A. (2014). *Far from the Tree: Parents, Children and the Search for Identity*. New York: Scribner.

Solomon, M., Miller, M., Taylor, S. L., Hinshaw, S. P., & Carter, C. S. (2012). Autism symptoms and internalising psychopathology in girls and boys with autism spectrum disorders. *Journal of Autism and Developmental Disorders*, 42, 48–59. doi: 10.1007/s10803-011-1215-z

Stagg, S. D., & Belcher, H. (2019). Living with autism without knowing: receiving a diagnosis in later life. *Health Psychology and Behavioral Medicine*, 7(1), 348–361. doi: 10.1080/21642850.2019.1684920

Stuart-Fox, S., & Moussalli, A. (2008). Selection for social signalling drives the evolution of chameleon colour change. *PLoS Biology*, 6(1), 22–29.

Tang, Y. Y., Hölzel, B., & Posner, M. (2015). The neuroscience of mindfulness meditation. *Nature Reviews Neuroscience*, 16, 213–225. doi: 10.1038/nrn3916

Taylor, S. E. (1983). Adjustment to threatening events: A theory of cognitive adaptation. *American Psychologist*, 38(11), 1161–1173. doi: 10.1037/0003-066X.38.11.1161

Tierney, S., Burns, J., & Kilbey, E. (2016). Looking behind the mask: social coping strategies of girls on the autistic spectrum. *Research in Autism Spectrum Disorders*, 23, 73–83. doi: 10.1016/j.rasd.2015.11.013

van Baaren, R. B., Maddux, W. W., Chartrand, T. L., de Bouter, C., & van Knippenberg, A. (2003). It takes two to mimic: behavioral consequences of self-construals. *Journal of Personality and Social Psychology*, 84(5), 1093–1102. doi: 10.1037/0022-3514.84.5.1093

van Roekel, E., Scholte, R. H., & Didden, R. (2010). Bullying among adolescents with autism spectrum disorders: prevalence and perception. *Journal of Autism and Developmental Disorders*, 40(1), 63–73. doi: 10.1007/s10803-009-0832-2

Willey, L. H. (1999). *Pretending to be Normal: Living with Asperger's Syndrome*. London: Jessica Kingsley Publishers.

Williams, D. (1998). *Nobody Nowhere: The Remarkable Autobiography of an Autistic Girl*. London: Jessica Kingsley Publishers.

Wiltermuth, S. S., & Heath, C. (2009). Synchrony and cooperation. *Psychological Science*, 20(1), 1–5. doi: 10.1111/j.1467-9280.2008.02253.x

Further Reading

For autistic adults

Bargiela, D. (2019). *Camouflage: The Hidden Lives of Autistic Women*. London: Jessica Kingsley Publishers.

Gilbert, P. (2010). *The Compassionate Mind*. London: Constable & Robinson.

Goodall, E., & Nugent, J. (2016). *The Guide to Good Mental Health on the Autism Spectrum*. London: Jessica Kingsley Publishers.

Sedgewick, F., Hull, L., & Ellis, H. (2021). *Autism and Masking: How and Why People Do It, and the Impact It Can Have*. London: Jessica Kingsley Publishers.

Van der Kolk, B. (2015). *The Body Keeps the Score: Mind, Brain and Body in the Transformation of Trauma*. London: Penguin.

Willey, L. H. (2014). *Pretending to Be Normal: Living with Asperger's Syndrome*. London: Jessica Kingsley Publishers.

For autistic children

Bonnello, C. (2019). *Underdogs*. London: Unbound Digital.

Lovegrove, E. (2020). *Autism, Bullying and Me: The Really Useful Stuff You Need to Know About Coping Brilliantly with Bullying*. London: Jessica Kingsley Publishers.

Morton, C., & Morton, G. (2015). *Why Johnny Doesn't Flap: NT Is OK!* London: Jessica Kingsley Publishers.

O'Neill, P. (2018). *Don't Worry, Be Happy: A Child's Guide to Dealing with Feeling Anxious*. London: Summersdale Publishers.

Purkis, Y., & Masterman, T. (2020). *The Awesome Autistic Go-To Guide: A Practical Handbook for Autistic Teens and Tweens*. London: Jessica Kingsley Publishers.

The Students of Limpsfield Grange School, & Martin. V. (2015). *M is for Autism*. London: Jessica Kingsley Publishers.

For parents/guardians

Ali, A. (2013). *A Practical Guide to Mental Health Problems in Children with Autistic Spectrum: It's Not Just Their Autism!* London: Jessica Kingsley Publishers.

Cat, S. (2018). *PDA by PDAers: From Anxiety to Avoidance and Masking to Meltdowns*. London: Jessica Kingsley Publishers.

Higashida, N. (2013). *The Reason I Jump*. London: Sceptre.

McCulloch, A., & McCulloch A. (2021). *Why Can't You Hear Me?: Our Autistic Daughter's Struggle to Be Understood*. London: Jessica Kingsley Publishers.

Silberman, S. (2017). *Neurotribes: The Legacy of Autism and How to Think Smarter About People Who Think Differently*. Sydney: Allen & Unwin.

Solomon, A. (2014). *Far From the Tree: Parents, Children and the Search for Identity*. New York: Scribner.

For educators

Gilbert. L., Gus, L., & Rose, J. (2021). *Emotion Coaching with Children and Young People in Schools: Promoting Positive Behaviour, Wellbeing and Resilience*. London: Jessica Kingsley Publishers.

Draisma, K. (2016). *Teaching University Students with Autism Spectrum Disorder: A Guide to Developing Academic Capacity and Proficiency*. London: Jessica Kingsley Publishers.

Hebron, J., & Bond, C. (2019). *Education and Girls on the Autism Spectrum: Developing an Integrated Approach*. London: Jessica Kingsley Publishers.

Truman, C. (2021). *The Teacher's Introduction to Pathological Demand Avoidance: Essential Strategies for the Classroom*. London: Jessica Kingsley Publishers.

For therapists

Ghaziuddin, M. (2005). *Mental Health Aspects of Autism and Asperger Syndrome*. London: Jessica Kingsley Publishers.

Moat, D. (2013). *Integrative Psychotherapeutic Approaches to Autism Spectrum Conditions: Working with Hearts of Glass*. London: Jessica Kingsley Publishers.

Subject Index

alexithymia 61, 74
anxiety 55–6
assimilation 40
authenticity in camouflaging 57–9
autism
   and camouflaging 31–4
   reasons for camouflaging 40–53
Autism and Masking: How and Why
   People Do It, and the Impact It
   Can Have (Sedgewick et al.) 19

Belcher, Dr Hannah Louise
   camouflaging experience 24–6, 49–50
   diagnosis of autism 16–17
   effects of camouflaging 54–5
   first autistic friend 52–3
   reducing camouflaging 111, 114,
      116, 118, 121, 123–4, 126, 128
   at school 15–16
   strategies for camouflaging 62–5
bullying 48–50

camouflaging
   author's experience of 24–6, 49–50
   and autism 31–4
   definition of 23
   developmental stages in 28–30
   effects of 54–60
   and gender 40–4
   reasons for 40–53
   reducing 109–37
   and social bonding 26–8
   strategies for 61–77
   traits of 36–40
Camouflaging Autistic Traits
   Questionnaire (CAT-Q)

definition of 35
effects of camouflaging 55
elements of camouflaging 36–7
gender in 41–2
strategies for camouflaging 66–70
Centre for Clinical Interventions (CCI) 101
'Chameleon Effect' 30–1
Cognitive Adaption Model
   definition of 109
   and reducing camouflaging 132–7
cognitive behavioural therapy (CBT)
   definition of 61
   and strategies for camouflaging 73
   and thinking errors 88
Compassionate Mind, The (Gilbert) 81
compensation
   definition of 35
   description of 39
Complete Guide to Asperger's Syn-
   drome, The (Attwood) 31

developmental stages 28–30
dialectic behaviour therapy (DBT)
   definition of 79
   in distress tolerance 94–101
distress tolerance
   definition of 79
   and self-compassion 94–101

effects of camouflaging 54–60
empathy
   and camouflaging 33–4
   definition of 23
executive functions
   definition of 35

executive functions *cont.*
  and gender 46
  and reasons for camouflaging 44–7
experimenting with camouflage
    reduction 120–32

gender
  and camouflaging 40–4
  in CAT-Q 41–2
  and executive functions 46

Hamm, Katherina 81, 105
Hendrickx, Sarah 31

identity and effects of cam-
    ouflaging 57–9
imagery work 103–7
imitation
  and 'Chameleon Effect' 30–1
  definition of 23
  degrees of 30–1

masking
  definition of 23
  description of 39
  at school 15–16
Mind Over Mood (Greenberger
    & Padesky) 91
mindfulness techniques 101–4

Neurotribes (Silberman) 52

phenotypes 35, 40
places for camouflaging 71–2
*Presentation of Self in Everyday
    Life, The* (Goffman) 47
Pretending to be Normal (Wiley) 24

radical acceptance 96
reasons for camouflaging
  bullying 48–50
  executive functions 44–7
  and gender 40–4

stigma avoidance 47–53
reducing camouflaging
  author's experience of 111, 114, 116,
    118, 121, 123–4, 126, 128
  and Cognitive Adaption
    Model 109, 132–7
  experimenting with 120–32
  rebuilding self in 132–7
  reconnecting with own
    happiness 110–20
  and stimming 115–16

Sapiens (Harari) 27
school, masking at 15–16
selective mutism 23
self-compassion
  and distress tolerance 94–101
  imagery work 103–7
  importance of 80–4
  mindfulness techniques 101–4
  thinking errors 85–92
social bonding 26–8
Somebody Somewhere (Williams) 53
stigma 47–53
stimming
  definition of 35
  and reducing camouflaging 115–16
  suppressing 39, 44, 66, 76
strategies for camouflaging
  author's experience of 62–5
  and CAT-Q 66–70
  exercise for 72–6
  time and place for camouflaging 70–1
suicidal behaviours 56
suppressing stimming 39, 44, 66, 76

theory of mind
  and camouflaging 33–4
  developmental stages in 29
thinking errors
  definition of 79
  and self–compassion 85–92
thwarted belonging 56
times for camouflaging 71–2

Author Index

Asendorpf, J. B. 29
Ashworth, F. 83
Attwood, T. 31

Bagatell, N. 57
Bailenson, J. N. 30
Baldwin, S. 41
Bargh, J. A. 30
Baron-Cohen, S. 43, 47
Baumeister, R. 29
Beck, A. T. 73, 121
Belcher, H. L. 51, 112
Bellebaum, C. 46
Bem, S. L. 42
Bird, G. 33
Bolte, S. 46
Bundy, R. 55
Burns, J. 46

Cage, E. 71
Carpenter, M. 30
Cassidy, S. 44, 56
Chartrand, T. L. 30
Cooper, K. 58
Costley, D. 41

Daum, I. 46
Dean, M. 42
Didden, R. 49
Dorstyn, D. 102
Due, C. 102

Ellis, A. 88
Estow, S. 31

Farley, J. 116

Fine, C. 42
Freud, S. 84

Gilbert, P. 27, 81, 82, 84, 103
Gillberg, C. 40
Goffman, E. 47, 48, 59
Greenberger, D. 91

Happé, F. 37
Harari, Y. N. 27
Hartley, M. 102
Harwood, R. 42
Hayes, S. C. 96
Heath, C. 71
Hendrickx, S. 31
Hollocks, M. J. 48
Hölzel, B. K. 102
Hull, L. 35, 36, 37, 42, 43,
     46, 55, 58, 66, 70

Ickes, W. 31

Jamieson, P. 31

Kapp, S. K. 115
Kasari, C. 42
Kilbey, E. 46
Kingstone, A. 116
Klimecki, O. 83
Kopp, S. 40

Lai, M. -C. 46
Lawson, W. 37
Leith, K. P. 29
Linehan, M. M. 94

Little, L. 48
Livingston, L. 37, 42, 46, 56

Makison, J. 30
Mandy, W. 11, 41
Marchant, J. 103
McGuigan, N. 30
Meltzoff, A. N. 28–9
Milton, D. 33
Morrison, K. E. 51
Moussalli, A. 15

Nadel, J. 28
National Autistic Society (NAS) 49

Office of National Statistics (ONS) 123
Otterman, D. L. 45
Ozonoff, S. 45

Padesky, C. A. 91
Pelton, M. K. 56
Pennington, B. 45
Piaget, J. 28

Reddan, M. C. 103
Risko, E. F. 116
Russell, A. 58

Sasson, N. 50, 51, 52
Schiller, D. 103

Scholte, R. H. 49
Sedgewick, F. 19, 42
Shonin, E. 101
Silberman, S. 52
Smith, L. G. E. 58
Solomon, M. 41, 57
Stagg, S. D. 112
Strosahl, K. D. 96
Stuart-Fox, S. 15

Tang, Y. Y. 102
Taylor, S. E. 132
Tierney, S. 46
Troxell-Whitman, Z. 71

van Baaren, R. B. 31
van Roekel, E. 49
Viding, E. 33

Wager, T. D. 103
Whiten, A. 30
Wiley, L. H. 24
Williams, D. 53
Wilson, K. G. 96
Wiltermuth, S. S. 71

Yates, J. R. 31
Yee, N. 30, 38

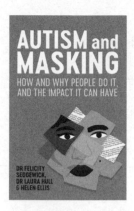

Autism and Masking
How and Why People Do It, and the Impact It Can Have
Dr Felicity Sedgewick, Dr Laura Hull and Helen Ellis

£16.99 | $24.95 | PB | 272pp | ISBN 978 1 78775 579 6 | eISBN 978 1 78775 580 2

Autistic people often feel they have to present as neurotypical or perform neurotypical social behaviours in order to fit in. So-called 'masking' is a social survival strategy used by autistic people in situations where neurodiversity is not understood or welcomed. While this is a commonly observed phenomenon in the autistic community, the complexities of masking are still not widely understood.

This book combines the latest research with personal case studies detailing autistic experiences of masking. It explains what masking is and the various strategies used to mask in social situations. The research also delves into the psychology behind masking and the specifics of masking at school, at social events with peers, and at work. The book looks at the consequences of masking, including the toll it can have on mental and physical health, and suggests guidance for family, professionals, and employers to ameliorate negative effects.

With a diverse range of voices, including perspectives across gender, ethnicity and age, this is the comprehensive guide to masking and how to support autistic people who mask.

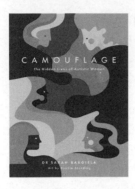

Camouflage
The Hidden Lives of Autistic Women
Dr Sarah Bargiela
Illustrated by Sophie Standing

£12.99 | $18.95 | HB | 48pp | ISBN 978 1 78592 566 5 |
eISBN 978 1 78592 667 9

Autism in women and girls is still not widely understood, and is often misrepresented or even overlooked. This graphic novel offers an engaging and accessible insight into the lives and minds of autistic women, using real-life case studies.

The charming illustrations lead readers on a visual journey of how women on the spectrum experience everyday life, from metaphors and masking in social situations, to friendships and relationships and the role of special interests.

Fun, sensitive and informative, this is a fantastic resource for anyone who wishes to understand how gender affects autism, and how to create safer supportive and more accessible environments for women on the spectrum.

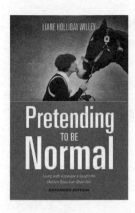

Pretending to be Normal
Living with Asperger's Syndrome (Autism Spectrum Disorder) Expanded Edition
Liane Holliday Willey

£14.99 | $21.95 | PB | 192pp | ISBN 978 1 84905 755 4 | eISBN 978 0 85700 987 6

Compelling and witty, Liane Holliday Willey's account of growing to adulthood as an undiagnosed 'Aspie' has been read by thousands of people on and off the autism spectrum since it was first published in 1999. Bringing her story up to date, including her diagnosis as an adult, and reflecting on the changes in attitude over 15 years, this expanded edition will continue to entertain (and inform) all those who would like to know a little more about how it feels to spend your life 'pretending to be normal'.

Safeguarding Autistic Girls
Strategies for Professionals
Carly Jones MBE
Foreword by Dr Luke Beardon

£19.99 | $27.95 | PB | 240pp | ISBN 978 1 787757 59 2 | eISBN 978 1 78775 760 8

This honest, to-the-point guide illuminates the experience of young Autistic girls and explores the situations they can easily fall victim to.

Powerful case studies show how easily misunderstandings can arise for Autistic girls and help the reader to identify common patterns of abuse.

Providing professionals with access to safeguarding strategies that are straightforward to implement and highly effective, this is essential reading for everyone who wants to better understand the challenges faced by this vulnerable group, and ensure they have access to the same opportunities to secure a good education and build safe and happy relationships as their peers.